Strawberry Hills Forever

Strawberry Hills Forever

Vanessa Berry

LCP local consumption publications

First published in 2007
Local Consumption Publications
Sydney Australia
www.localconsumption.com

Berry, Vanessa, 1978– .
Strawberry Hills Forever.

ISBN 978-0-949-793-32-4 (pbk.)

1. Berry, Vanessa. 2. Autobiography. I. De Souza, Keg.
II. Title.

Cover design and typesetting by Pat Armstrong
Printed and bound in Australia by McPhersons Printing Group

Australian Government

Australia Council for the Arts

This project has been assisted by the Australian Government through the Australia Council, its principal arts funding and advisory body.

For Natasha Smith and Stephanie Varga.

Contents

Strawberry Hills Forever

Occasionally people write me letters in which they imagine what Strawberry Hills is like. They describe fields and fruits and cottages and so obviously have no knowledge of Sydney. I once received a postcard covered in drawings of strawberries and the message, 'I grow strawberries in my garden'. I looked up from the thin pencil lines on the card to Strawberry Hills post office, a large, salmon-coloured office building among the tired terraces of Redfern and Surry Hills. The only berry in sight was me.

I like that people are inspired to imagine what Strawberry Hills must be like, that this is something they give me in exchange for what I give them in my zines. Like their image of Strawberry Hills, the way they imagine me from my writing is probably as fantastic. Reading my zines and letters, they build their own version of me and vice versa. I love this idea: that we all have lives different to our real ones in other people's minds.

Hundreds, possibly thousands, of envelopes have come through my post office box. They are as varied as the people who send them, neat or ragged or crisp or gorgeous. They are exciting because they are very personal objects, with obvious traces of their origin and the journey they have taken to reach my hands. They are always idiosyncratic and in some way imperfect: a letter will never reach its destination exactly as it left it.

One thing that frustrates me about books is that the authors often seem so removed from them. Books are encountered as seamless objects, with only scraps at the beginning and end to give clues about how it came into being. Finishing a book I enjoy I often feel disappointed by its impermeability. I consider that writing to the author might help but I don't like the idea of sending a letter through a publisher. This seems too much like writing a fan letter. It never feels like the right thing to do because it suggests I want to befriend the author, or expect a personal acknowledgement from them.

What I do crave is for books themselves to have looser boundaries, to be less discrete and reverential objects. The feeling that I so often miss is one of reciprocity, that by reading I am pulled into a dialogue with an author, rather than distantly experiencing their words. This doesn't mean that the subject matter has to be particularly personal; certain fiction can make me feel this way and certain non fiction can make me feel the opposite. This feeling of reciprocity is one I always feel with zines, which is why I love them, even if the content doesn't interest me. I just love that they exist. Making zines has changed the way I read. Now, no matter how much I enjoy reading books, I cannot stop myself from wishing they were a bit more like the envelopes that come through my post box.

I hope that I have managed to retain these feelings of reciprocity and personal communication in *Strawberry Hills Forever.* Many of the stories within first appeared in my zines, but all were written with the same intention: to share something with you, to send you a letter.

So, until next time, I remain yours,

Vanessa Berry
PO Box 1879
Strawberry Hills NSW 2012
Australia

Adventures

instead of a mirror,

i use the faces of the people
we pass on the street

Violet Slaughter

1.

Violet came to me via the post, in tiny envelopes bearing my name in dagger-like script. The typewritten pages inside had the rushed, unpunctuated appearance of telegrams. Rattled out in great passion, they pulled me into her life.

I found her through the whimsical world of underground publishing. I'd started writing zines with the same verve I employed on projects in primary school. My desk, recently liberated from high-school study notes, became host to hundreds of cut outs I clipped from magazines and newspapers my boyfriend brought home from the recycling bin at his call-centre job. I cut out anything that was worthy of my derision, glued them around the edges of a folded sheet of paper, and scrawled whatever came into my head in the gap. I called the result 'Psychobabble' and left copies in the doorway of Waterfront Records, for people to pick up along with the street press and the flyers for bands that would either explode or wither. Reading them now feels like finding an old letter I never expected to see again. They're slapdash and my rounded script looks childish.

At the same time I was cutting through newspapers, Violet explained that she had been 'imprisoned' on a farm an hour away from Wagga Wagga the whole of the summer, with only her parents for company. In her first letter she explained how she had survived:

> *I killed isolation and nervous guilt through writing and the pseudo perfection of my record collection.*

I ordered her zine, *Bad Turnip Man*, from Spiral Objective, a mail order catalogue that compiled dense lists of zines and punk records. It was exciting to receive the catalogue in the post and squint through the grids of items typed in a tiny font. I'd been attracted to *Bad Turnip Man* because it promised 'The Church, PJ Harvey and Gardening Tips'. When I received the zine I read the rest of the contents list: 'Inarticulate Poems, Reviews, Bitterness, Joy Division, Crossword, Naivety, Elvis Costello and How to build your own guillotine from rice paper!!!'

By contrast *Psychobabble #1* had promised 'Shite B-Grade Films, Self Indulgence, How to get Mail and Friends, Sex drugs and SIN, Life Philosophy, Zine Reviews and My favourite things.' I listed my favourite names from the Bible and scoffed at a Cleo article I read waiting in line at Franklins called 'The Lazy Girls Guide to Sex'. Where I had cynicism, Violet had vitriol and a curious vernacular. I read her zine in one sitting and reaching the end I felt as if I had surfaced after swimming in a viscid dream world:

> *My nerves are giving me the wind up symbol, the ecstasy is starting to fade. Yes chums it's FIN. I hope someone reads this. By the time this is circulating the zygote of nauseating regret will probably be old enough to be in the prom video, all the places in*

town with photocopiers will be locked or will only do onesided etc.
Most of this I hate, but I must admit the foreign zest experienced
at the typewriter was welcome before it got bored and left me.

After these last words, I craved more. I had the feeling I had discovered something limited and precious, almost by chance. I found out later that the only place in town she could find with a photocopier was the Catholic church, so her zine emerged from the same machine as the Saturday-night mass sheets. She only made twenty-five copies.

I spent a day constructing my letter to her. Form was important. I used black fountain pen on grainy grey paper with a rearing unicorn stamped in the corner. I'd kept this notepaper for years and only used it for special letters. I hinted that we were probably soulmates and listed all we shared. Both of us wanted to be Sylvia Plath, our lives had been saved by music, we expressed ourselves in messy cut and paste, we felt isolated and lonely and wrote to fill in the gaps.

I sent the letter from the GPO, a grand building that made me think of affairs held via post boxes in the 1920s. It felt right to be posting this important letter there. I thought of the letter's journey and by the end of the week, knowing she would have it, I could imagine her fingers at the envelope and myself appearing in front of her as a ghostly sister. She took a month to reply, a time in which I constructed endless conversations with her as if she were beside me. I'd dropped out of university and my life felt aimless unless I was writing letters.

Violet was embedded in a Wollongong University college. Due to a clerical mishap she was assigned a room in the sports college, adjacent to the athletics fields. The rooms were cells with tiny windows, and the sound of footsteps and giggling from the hallway was incessant. Giant, lanky boys pummelled the hallways like running bulls, trying door handles to see if they could catch undressed girls or couples engaging in one of the many intra-college liasons.

In her first letter, she listed the reasons why she was on the verge of being kicked out:

> *1. because our college head friendly phil hates bhp cadets and goths. 2. because I like to cut my wrists. 3. because I like to wear 'unnerving' white face paint. 4. because I'm a 'psycho' 5. because I am antisocial.*

On the back of the letter were three photocopied photographs. The third was taken in a suburban lounge room. The backdrop is a long curtain that I don't need to see in colour to know it is shades of yellow, brown and pink. In front of it stands a guy with thick caterpillar eyebrows and sunglasses on his head. Beside him is Violet, looking askance at the camera, her face the whitest part of the photograph, hair curving down the side of her cheek as if drawn in black ink. The outline of a feather boa bursts from her black coat. At the left of the picture is the flannelette back of another guy. I never found out where this photo was taken, so I don't know whether the guy was one of the despised 'sportos' or not, or why she was standing so exotically among yobbos in a living room.

Her face looked different in every photo. In the first she is wearing what looked to be a wedding dress, holding a posy of baby's breath. I found out later this photo was from what she referred to as 'the prom' and everyone else called 'the Year 12 formal'. 'The prom' was a reference to *Carrie* and she had expected, perhaps, the same gory punishment wreaked upon her as upon Carrie in the film. Crazed, drenched in blood and seething with the shame of unpopularity.

In the middle photo she's playing a guitar in front of a cluttered chest of drawers. The drawers are hanging open and leaking clothes, the surfaces are cluttered with cosmetics. I looked for clues among this clutter. I stared into these photographs with the same attention I examined pictures of the notable people I wanted to be. Sad female poets, angry female singers, wistful muses. I thought if I stared enough, I'd absorb something of them and my life would follow a similar path. With these pictures the feeling was different. She wasn't an antelope-legged Anne Sexton in an op-art halter dress, or Polly Harvey sneering with all the anger of a girl disgusted by men. She was real and I'd found her.

We arranged to meet at Central station, in the lofty building containing the country platforms. This part of Central station resembles an aircraft hangar; whenever I'm in there I picture 747s being disembowelled by mechanics. To make a dramatic impression I had dressed carefully in black lace and dangled myself with silver jewellery. I tried to style myself as close to my ideal as possible, although it was difficult. I idolised the dream-image of ethereal girls with dark hair, dressed in lace and rags. I wanted to look post apocalyptic, in boots and ripped stockings, draped in spiderweb fabric.

The few other people waiting had taken up seats and were leaned against ticket machines, compulsively checking their watches. If these people wait as long as me, I thought, it will be alright, she will come. But it was getting later and the faces of the people around me split into recognition one by one, they swiftly joined their friends and moved on. I watched the hands of the clock shudder forwards with every minute. The crowd didn't part to reveal her and everyone looked dull and anonymous, either charging home after work or sandbagged by giant backpacks.

I didn't know what to do. I'd invested all my hope into our moment of meeting. I continued waiting because I couldn't think of anything else to do. I had an intuitive feeling that from this point in my life, everything would be different. Meeting her would change things. But now I felt bruised, disappointed that my premonition was nothing but the side effect of wishful thinking.

I had been there for an hour when I saw her among the grey shoulders of commuters. She was wearing a brown lace dress that reminded me of funerals and curtains. I noticed with disappointment that there were two people with her, a lumbering guy and a girl with sharp cheekbones and calculating eyes. I had imagined our meeting to be a kind of reunion, where words rushed out of us as easily as they did in our letters, but the presence of the others caught me off guard. She introduced them as Amy and Stamos and we stood uncomfortably for a moment, unsure of what to say to each other.

We boarded a train to the northern suburbs. The mood was awkward and frosty, the three of them were locked in a conspiracy that I could not join. I tried not to let my discomfort show and cast sly looks at Violet, fascinated by her appearance. She was much shorter than me, with giant blue eyes ringed in black eyeliner. Her fingernails were coated with layers of black and red polish, as if the old, chipped polish was never removed, only more added over the top, giving her fingers a busy, uncaring look, like the paint stained fingers of an artist.

I could have made small talk, pointed to the letters scratched out of the notices inside the train carriage – 'at night rave near the guard's compartment naked with a blue light' – but the lack of importance of these things was too obvious. I didn't want to prattle like I was escorting my aunt and uncle who'd just come from interstate. Stamos stared out the window at the harbour as we crossed the bridge, while Amy said odd, arch things as if she had just acted in a school play and refused to get out of character. I didn't like her.

She complained about the distance we had to walk from the station and kept doing strange things with her hands and ranting about the third eye, and how she needed to find a field so she could 'focus'. I could tell that Amy delighted in her oddness but it made me weary. I'd been usurped by more confident and charismatic people all my life, and I despaired that it was happening again.

After what felt like an unusually long time we reached Matt's ugly bachelor apartment. It was built to withstand the ravages of tenants, therefore it could never feel homely. The bathroom was the size of a broom cupboard, the ceiling low, the carpet made of tough strands of cream and brown, designed to camouflage dirty footprints.

With Amy and Stamos there I felt I could hardly get through to Violet. They were a couple of mismatched chaperones and I was mute in their presence. They buzzed like static. Stamos showed us the scars from his lobotomy operation, matching ridges on each of his temples. He had a soft, flat, American accent and, conforming to my limited knowledge of lobotomies, was particularly emotionless. Outside on the balcony Amy recited lines from *Equus*. Violet and I sat together on the carpet, leaning back against the couch on which Stamos reclined. We were drinking vodka from plastic cups patterned with characters from The Simpsons. It was the time of night where all around the city, kids would be drinking their nightly glass of milk from the same garish receptacles.

The people from the apartment above kept knocking at the door, pleading for quiet. I could hear Amy outside, conversing with the tangle of weeds between the balcony and the neighbour's fence. I felt a spiralling, out of control feeling because these strangers had taken over. I didn't know Stamos' real name, only that Violet called him this because he resembled a more lacklustre and heavyset John Stamos from *Full House*. In fact, I didn't even know *her* real name, unless she had really been christened Violet Slaughter.

We were nervous together. I could feel the warmth of her upper arm, pressing against mine. She was tense and trembling, her words tumbled and hissed, and she had a rapturous laugh, wide and beguiling. When she laughed I could feel the air around us ripping. On this dull landscape, littered with secondhand furniture that still held the ghosts of strangers' bodies, I saw us as two daubs of oil paint, slick and rich.

Our meeting had been structured around seeing The Church that night. A month earlier she had written me a note suggesting that we should go to the concert together. From the start, our correspondence had been pregnant with our eventual meeting, so it was a relief to have her suggest it.

Much of our communion had arisen through our shared musical taste. Violet adored the Church's oblique lyrics and layers of hypnotic, music-box guitar, but I knew little about them before I met her. To prepare for the concert

I compulsively listened to the tape Violet had sent me of her favourite Church songs. The frightening, otherworldly 'Shadow Cabinet' was my favourite, the song she described:

> *It seems to skip along innocently enough but when set to a gothic background of a twilight forest with blood-drained, grey fairies being dragged by their enchanted feet, a sense of strange, nightmarish security lingers over it all. When you write their songs phonetically, it is like you have to write it in stars.*

Her language was mesmerising, idiosyncratic. I longed to understand it, but I also enjoyed its incomprehensibility. I felt I was at sea among a mysterious landscape.

Amy came back in and complained about the music. She had specific songs she wanted to hear, none of which we owned, a fact which disgusted her. She crouched over the milk crate of records and flipped through them. While she was occupied, arguing with Matt over his taste in LPs, Violet and I slipped out onto the balcony. She whispered that she and Amy had taken acid that afternoon, and she felt 'autistic' and without control. I promised I would look after her and we embraced, furtively, as if we risked being caught. She smelt of rose oil, cigarette smoke, talcum powder and old cloth. It was the same scent that clung to her letters and it mystified me. Previously I'd only ever known girls who smelt of Impulse and lip gloss.

Inside, Stamos patted the pockets of his brown leather jacket and announced, 'I have to go. I forgot to bring my medication.' He looked relieved to have come across this excuse. Despite concerns he wouldn't be able to find his way back to the train station, he insisted that he needed to leave straight away.

We left soon after. Matt drove us to the station in his two-seater station wagon. Amy and Violet perched in the back, among the debris and ropes and crumpled copies of *The Drum Media*. They were speaking to each other in

French, passionately accenting the smooth syllabled words. I was terrified that they were speaking about me, and had to hide their dislike in the unfamiliar phrases of another language. I slouched against the cracked vinyl of the seat, listening to their voices and hating feeling excluded. The streaky neons of kebab stores and furniture warehouses trailed past outside the window. I was tipsy and everything far away was blurry, everything close appeared magnified.

We parked crookedly across two car spaces in the train station parking lot. 'That'll do,' Matt shrugged drunkenly. By the time we sat waiting for the train Amy and Violet had given up on French, and I shyly discussed my hopes for the Church concert, feeling dreadfully pedestrian for being so realistic.

Trains at night give me a lost feeling, travelling through darkness in an illuminated cell full of strangers. They make me feel exposed, as if I'm sitting in a giant x-ray machine and anyone can see right through me. I pressed myself into the corner, away from the windows. After a few stops Amy stood up and announced she was going home. Without waiting to be convinced otherwise, she turned and disappeared down the carriage steps.

I was glad to be rid of her; it was as if a spell had been lifted. Amy's warped charisma frightened me. The nervous coils of worry in my stomach unfurled and dissolved. Despite our moment of communion on the balcony, I had been worried that Amy was the type of person Violet was really attracted to, and I couldn't compete with her spiky strangeness. I felt it *was* a competition and that Violet was the prize for my choice of passion over sense, in this year after high school where my school friends had joined the moving walkway to success in high-paid careers, and I chose making magazines with scissors and glue and writing letters to alluring strangers. If I'd chosen correctly, I'd have Violet as a soulmate.

I'd spent the last ten years at a private girls' school, where competition laced every possible exchange. Everything had to be fought for, especially where friends were concerned. I knew the heavy hearted feeling of rejection that came from a girl I idolised snubbing my attentions. I'd learnt that female friendships had to be fought for and maintained. They were far more nuanced and exciting than relationships with boys, who at the time seemed like completely different creatures.

We had to travel across town, to Coogee. I'd never been there before, but I knew it to be a haunt of English backpackers that featured little but a beach and its associated culture. The show was at Selinas, a dark barn of a room, where the majority of the audience were the blue-jeaned, Longbeach smoking type. It wasn't the collection of fragile souls we had expected, but we at least had the distraction of following the early-80s Steve Kilbey (or Steve Giblet as Violet called him for some unknown reason) lookalike who had been seated in front of us on the bus. Our aim was to get a photo:

> *We were two hours late but still two hours early and we had effectively camouflaged ourselves into the wall when he walked past. Then the sadistic, smug, condescending 'smile next time' i.d. verifiant coldly indicated that cameras were not allowed and it was in my best interest to surrender it to the cloakroom. So I did but it was like I had one foot each on two pieces of ice that were rapidly drifting apart. He walked past again. Surely three fatal indications were too skull-marked to ignore? I quickly decided that dying under the blow of his dry and delicate hand was excessively desirable and gushed, '*Excuse me. *Are you aware that you bear a striking resemblance to Steve Giblet? Would you strongly object to being photographed for warmth and status?'*

He shyly accepted, and she baptised him in the flash from her old, boxy camera, before handing it over to the cloakroom staff. We found a place among a sea of louts at the front of the stage. People around us sloshed beer over the rims of their cups and a cacophony of anticipatory hoots rose and fell, until the lights dimmed.

We still imagined the band as they'd appeared in videos from the early eighties: waif-like, in velvet coats, ambling through a winter forest. Twelve years on their appearance shocked us. Steve Kilbey was dressed in denim with greying hair in a ponytail, the visual equivalent of his world weary in-between song banter. All of them except Marty Willson-Piper looked as if the last five years had been difficult. At least Marty looked as if he'd been preserved in ice since the velvet coat era, Violet whispered joyfully.

Despite their tired appearance, the band performed with the magic that had enraptured me on their albums. I was swept up by the immediacy of the songs I had memorised from cassettes. I could tell Violet felt the same, we held hands and exchanged squeezes, understanding each other without speaking. I finally felt what I had hoped for from our meeting; cast adrift from my normal life, in an unfamiliar place with this magical girl.

If only we hadn't been surrounded by philistines. The blonde girl beside us squealed 'this has been my New Year's theme song since I was eighteen!' at the opening lines of 'Under the Milky Way', the stubble-jawed Neanderthal nearby grumbled every time they slowed the tempo and subdued the volume. These were not the kindred spirits we had hoped would surround us. Kindred were defined by their pain at the vulgarity of existence, they shunned conventional pleasures and interests, they were sun-starved and insomniac and their fingers had writers' calluses. How could the boorish mass at Selinas like the same music as us?

After the encore the house lights glared on and the crowd dispersed. We stumbled over the empty beer cans that covered the floor, looking for Matt. To my embarrassment he was asleep in a corner, but he quickly shook himself awake and we spilled out onto the street. Drunk backpackers gnawed kebabs and chewed with their mouths open. The bins were overflowing, cups and packets had spilled onto the ground beneath them in petticoats of trash. The ocean was indistinguishable, a huge black blot to our right. I imagined it as a hell from which these monsters around us had crawled.

The bus timetable was redundant; it had ceased to be useful hours before. For all its 11.44s and 9.57s, it was now past midnight and nothing could save us but a taxi. I watched the meter, it seemed to add a cent per turn of the wheels. I could never be cool enough not to worry about money. Violet couldn't either. 'I've got no money,' she whispered, suddenly small and frightened. 'I can't get home.'

'Stay with me,' I said, as we rested our lacy shoulders against the cushioned interior of the taxi and ignored the driver's questions about whether it had been a good night. The trip was long and expensive and it was 2 am by the time we arrived at my house.

Roused by our return, my dressing-gowned mother constructed the camp bed with the orange sunburst 70s mattress on my bedroom floor and placed a wedge of fresh sheets on it, before disappearing back to bed. My room seemed awfully quiet after the concert, I put on 'Faith' by The Cure on low volume and we whispered to each other over its sparse, cathedral sound.

I knew that Violet wasn't her real name. The address in her zine was 'Violet Slaughter c/o Miss N. Smith', and these two identities intrigued me. I had suspicions about Miss N. Smith, which were solidified when Amy had farewelled her on the train. I waited until I was home to try out her real name.

'Natasha?'

She looked disappointed.

Natasha never cared too much for reality or facts, for her everything was mutable. While I found her real name important, she was dismissive of the importance of this fact. In her world people could choose their own names as they wished. Perhaps this started during her isolated upbringing when she had to rely on music for solace and companionship. The magazines and fanzines she read presented personas and characters that rejected the mundane and everyday. Why should it be any different for us? We could self mythologise without waiting for fame.

I craved myths as a way to escape. I lived in a post-war brick box with my mother and sister, on a street where houses like ours were slowly being demolished and replaced with two-storey project homes. I never spoke to any of the local kids and their parents looked at me strangely because of the way I dressed. I felt as out of place here as I had at school; I was only there because of a bursary and although my family were middle class, I felt poor compared to the other ultra-rich students.

In the morning Natasha woke up much earlier than me and disappeared to the bathroom to put on makeup. She worked hard to conceal her red hair and freckles. When her red roots became visible and she couldn't afford dye she sometimes painted over the roots with shoe polish, she hated them so much. Her skin disappeared underneath layers of pale foundation and powder which she was meticulous in maintaining.

While Natasha was in my room reading a biography of Ian Curtis and I was making toast in the kitchen, my mother took me aside. She whispered that the bathroom was a terrible mess, covered in white powder. I went to investigate the source of the trouble – the tiles were powdery, but easily cleaned. My mother had an objection to talcum powder. Whenever I was given powder as a gift from my cousins as a child (Christmas brought either powder, bubble bath in cartoon character-shaped receptacles, or singlet and underpants sets) it languished at the back of the bathroom cabinet, unused.

I wiped away some of the powder with a face washer, but scooped up the long black hairs that lined the sink to keep as a souvenir. Evidence was very important, business cards, napkins and notes made me feel I existed. I still kept used train tickets in a biscuit tin.

Later, after Natasha caught the train home I laid the long black hairs in between two pages of a notebook. I kept them for fear of never seeing her again because I hadn't proved myself worthy, or because I had dreamed her up out of desire for a soulmate.

2.

I first visited Natasha a month after the Church concert. I spent the two-hour train journey writing Plathesque poetry about being consumed by emotions as savage as white heat. I paid all my attention to my exercise book, ignoring the dramatic view of the ocean from the windows. The heads of the old couples who shared the carriage all turned to stare over the wide expanse of blue as they mumbled about its beauty. Having Natasha inspired me to admit I didn't care for the beauties of nature. I cared about the life of the mind, I didn't want to indulge in conventional pleasures like cooing at scenery.

Meanwhile, at the station, Natasha was being hassled by a man who wanted to talk about 'Gothics'. While she waited for my delayed train, he tried to engage her in discussions of clubbing and drug-taking in the 'Gothic' scene, thinking that would convince her that he was with-it. Really we were terrified of clubbing, of the immaculate looking goth girls who could afford proper cosmetics and knew how to apply them, who looked icy and otherworldly and existed on a diet of cigarettes and the odd handful of potato crisps.

We'd both been attracted to goth because it seemed the only subculture where it was acceptable to be intelligent and sensitive and luxuriate in melancholy. However the social side of it eluded us. My excursions to clubs were dominated by intense feelings of inadequacy. I never looked quite right and I felt painfully young compared to everyone else there. Natasha and I were bedroom goths. Our lives centred around rooms with walls covered in pictures, covert smoking of clove cigarettes, notebook scribbling and looking through messy piles of cassettes for the perfect song for that moment.

Seeing her waiting at the station I felt immense relief. She emerged from among travellers in khaki and T-shirts and we surged towards each other and embraced carefully, as if we were breakable. The man who had been talking to her melted away into a clump of polo shirts and sports bags. We fled the station and began the walk to the college.

In one of my first letters I'd asked her what she could see out her window. I told her of my uninspiring view of the back garden, sometimes interrupted by the heads of the children next door bouncing up over the side fence as they jumped on their trampoline, but otherwise static as a landscape painting.

> *My window looks out on a roof about a metre below me so that if I need to jump I will only be able to do so when its raining so I can be killed on a mountain spike piercing me a la stake through the heart…slipping down…then far far away I can see into the other cells but they are normally with blinds drawn, fairly useless, the windows only postage stamp sized.*

I had pictured the college as a grand place, but when we arrived it was a cluster of utilitarian blocks, like an outer suburban TAFE college. We rushed through a warren of hallways towards her tiny room. It was crammed full, pictures stuck all over the walls, cupboards bursting. There was nowhere to sit but the bed, her desk chair was covered in clothes and papers. I looked fondly upon the antique computer on which she wrote her letters, keyboard stained with splotches of hair dye and the sticky ghosts of coffee spills.

We turned the cassette of Christian Death's 'Only Theatre of Pain' up loud and got stuck into a bottle of Blackberry Nip as we refined our outfits for the impending meeting of the Wollongong Uni Gothic Society. Blackberry Nip is a sickly, cheap wine of teeth-rotting sweetness. We preferred sugary alcohol. Port was our other favourite, which for reasons of thrift we bought in 4-litre bottles. I hadn't done much drinking in my life and the excessive sugar content disguised the sharp taste.

The meeting was held at a cafe in town, a decidedly non-goth place with exposed brick walls and long rickety tables. To our disappointment most of the people attending looked drab, wearing black jeans and t-shirts. None of the friends Natasha enthused about in her letters – Andrew, Irene, Azriel – turned up. I was disappointed that I didn't meet these friends who played such a major role in her letters. We spent much of the night talking to the second bests, like Leo who was sitting across from us. Leo was a Nick Cave obsessive with pinched features and lank blue-black hair. He railed against Catholicism ad nauseam until we told him we had Virgin Mary complexes and he couldn't think of a reply. After a silence he noticed that both Natasha and I had scars on our arms, and this prompted him to take a photo of us proudly displaying our cut wrists. The camera flash seared our images onto film; I felt it sealed our friendship, it was evidence of our bond.

I have kept all my relics. When writing about our first meeting I looked through my suitcases of cassettes to find the first Church tape she sent me and played it on the same shoddy stereo on which I first heard it. Thousands of cassettes later the stereo looks battered and the sound is an anxiety inducing treble. Despite this, in listening I could remember the thrill of hearing it years ago, the feeling that Violet and this music would lead me on an adventure towards being the kind of person I wanted to be.

Looking through her letters, my heart feels heavy. I read through the dense pages and hear her voice in them. The words feel inflected with passion and dynamics, like the score of a violent, heart-seizing piece of music. Up until now I have mostly avoided thinking of the details of our friendship, afraid of the inevitable grief.

After she died of leukaemia in 1998 I no longer had any reason to visit Wollongong. Without her the city was bled of meaning. In my memory it became a fairy-tale place, presided over by the ominous escarpment. It was a town of crumbling streets, wide concrete drains and secret pathways through parks and vacant blocks. Our ghosts were everywhere.

Recently, when a friend was scheduled to give a talk at Wollongong University, I decided it was time to return. I arrived early so I could revisit the college where Natasha used to live.

I made my first wrong turn by choosing the footbridge that crossed the freeway. On the other side I stopped strangers and showed them the pathetic scrap of paper on which I'd written directions. The paper was limp from being clasped in my hand, I hoped that continually consulting it would imbue me with navigational prowess. The scrawled lines and street names corresponded to nothing around me. The food technology students with tackle boxes of knives couldn't help me, nor could the angry guy with 'Metallica' written in very small, neat letters on his backpack.

I didn't recognise anywhere that I was walking. Eventually I asked a bus driver and he annoyed his passengers by spending five minutes going over the best way to walk there. I peered over his shoulder at a grubby street directory, his jumper smelt faintly of kerosene. Following his directions I walked through unfamiliar suburban streets where there was no movement other than red leaves dropping from the liquidambar trees. It could have been anywhere until I turned onto the main road, and recognition bolted through me.

It was a feeling of unveiling, as if remembering a dream.

I passed the tennis courts where our outfits used to shock the players and make them miss their shots. Their eager figures bounced left and right like they were made of rubber bands. It looked exactly the same as it had on those days when they'd paused to stare as we promenaded past in black lace, fishnets and layers of petticoats.

The college itself was smaller than I remembered it. Standing at the entrance I had the same feeling as returning to a childhood playground, when suddenly everything looks shabby and miniature. A memorial tree had been planted in the front garden the day Natasha would have graduated, but when I searched for it there was only a succession of wiry banksias, and no plaque. The garden was choked with fallen leaves and mulch.

I walked around all the different buildings that made up the college. I could see the outlines of liquor bottles, soft toys and books through the small windows and hear excited yelling from the TV room. When I returned to the entrance, I ducked inside.

As soon as I entered the foyer, a girl at the reception desk asked if she could help me.

'I'm just having a look around.'

She was suspicious.

'I had a friend who lived here years ago, and I was in the area ...'

I didn't want to explain any further or inflict the thought of death upon her afternoon.

'Do you want to go in?' she smiled, opening the door to the main college building.

Immediately to my right was the dining room where Natasha and I used to eat creamy potatoes off one plate like Siamese twins. Students weren't allowed to bring friends in to eat without purchasing a meal ticket, but we tried our best to get around it. We were often caught, an extra goth stuck out. I'd try to sit behind a pole and slump down, but the grouchy cafeteria ladies with sparse, copper-rinsed hair and peevish expressions would usually spot me. Today the room was empty except for a group of students having a meeting.

I felt like even more of an impostor than I used to. Now I looked conspicuously old as well as strangely dressed. Some of the rooms had their doors wide open, girls in shorts lounged on single beds inside, reading magazines or doing their engineering homework. The doors had names on them, painted onto A4 sheets in rainbow colours, I walked down a row of Emilys, Melanies, Brads and other substantial, average names. Sporto girls and jocks hung out casually in the corridors, talking about getting drunk and having to be wheeled home in shopping trolleys. They hadn't changed.

There's no one at billcrosby college who I feel is worth me talking to, not saying I'm too good for them but we are just on utterly different planets.

I wanted to will myself back into 1996 and find her door, covered in pictures from music magazines and Rimbaud poems printed from the internet, to have her by my side, the key ready in her hand so we could get inside as quickly as possible. Inside, breathe in the familiar smell of crushed petals and cigarettes.

We were safe in her room, no longer threatened by the crude inhabitants of the hallways. The photographs of friends on her walls reminded us that beyond the walls of college, at least a few other people like us existed.

Natasha took her camera with her everywhere. At eighteen we knew we were destined for notoriety, so we needed as many photographs as possible to record our youth.

Although it was a pivotal memory, the photograph of us displaying our wrists at the Gothic Society dinner remained a mystery for a long time. The negative was at the start of a poorly wound-on roll of film and only half exposed, preventing photo labs from being able to print it. I found it when I was searching for another picture and knew it was the last photograph I would find of her. All the others had soaked into my memory, I had stared into them desperate for every last detail that might evoke her.

I asked Tim to print it in his home darkroom. He disappeared for a while into his blacked out, chemical-scented bathroom then called me in. I watched the picture floating in a tray of water. Her hands are reaching towards the camera, she looks as if she has an aversion to them and wants to push them as far away from her as possible. I have a sheepish smile, which I remembered regretting afterwards. Why couldn't I have looked haughty and dangerous? You can't see the cuts on either of our wrists and behind us looms the menu board: 'Gado Gado $5'. It wasn't nearly as rich or beautiful as the night had been in my memory.

The negative for this photo had been in my desk drawer for years, colliding with staples and paperclips, hence the print is spotted and scratched. On either side of us are white haloes from the exposed parts of the film, so we appear to be rising out of a fog. Seeing it I realised how my memories of Natasha have been clouded, dominated by photographs and letters as the years since her death increase.

It doesn't feel nine years ago, but at the same time it doesn't feel immediate either. Our friendship feels timeless, ingrained, as if it has always been a part of me. When I speak of her I want people to care intensely, but she is difficult to evoke. Most often I stay silent, and feel her absence like a lack of oxygen.

Relics

Church

Outside the church, a girl the height of my elbows was handing out thin candles from a plastic bag. I instinctively raised the candle to my nose; it smelt of wax crayons and pre-school. A group of priests were standing around a fire in a silver bowl. One held a bag of Jiffy firelighters, the others hovered with matches. This didn't seem very holy. In my romanticised expectations of church, fires spring forth when bidden, priests are never seen in jeans, nothing modern or practical intrudes. I am always disappointed. The girl who handed me the candle, for example, was wearing a robe coupled with oversized white sneakers, the type that remind me of obese bellies, all rolls and pouches.

The priests finished attending to the fire, satisfied that it would remain alight for long enough, and began the service. As the main priest gathered his voice and exhaled a greeting I ceased to pay attention. The two people standing behind me weren't interested in listening either, they were conducting a conversation in stage whispers:

'See that priest on the left? He was moved from this church last year. No one liked him, so they sent him away somewhere, the city I heard.'

'Which one, that one with the white–'

'No, next to him, the one with the skating rink.'

I was confused until I realised he was referring to the circular bald patch on the head of the unpopular priest.

The gossiping couple were distracted by the distribution of flame from the main fire to the candles held by the congregation. I lit my candle from those of a nearby family and cupped my palm around it to inspire the flame to take hold. Warm splatters of wax dripped onto my shoes and skirt as I followed everyone up the stairs into the church. I decided not to pretend I was a Catholic. I sometimes did, despite my secular upbringing, as I had a fascination with the rituals involved in the services. However this time I neither dipped my fingers in Holy Water to make the sign of the cross, nor bowed at the entrance to the pew, as the others around me did. I was frightened that they would think me a terrible heathen, but could not bring myself to pretend I believed in, or even really knew, the intricate rituals of the church.

The romance of church was further broken when the music started. For every musical interlude or response someone pressed a button on a tape recorder, which unleashed an electronic, karaoke-style version of the tune required. I found this almost unbearably embarrassing, far worse than the Jiffy firelighters and sneakers.

This church was where Natasha's funeral had been held. That day I found myself seated in between her parents in the front pew, I had been too numb and mute to protest or think of the consequences of this until after I was sitting down. I remember my hands shaking, clenched so tightly the knuckles looked blue, and a feeling of unbearable sickness. People around me were singing hymns but I was mute, I felt as if my heart had swollen to fill my chest and was straining against my ribs. I wasn't crying although I had stuffed my handbag with tissues in preparation. Funerals make every action horrible and small; putting on eyeliner, packing a handbag, walking to the car. When the service was over somebody nearby urgently whispered, 'Take her!', in case I fainted I suppose. A man with a bristly moustache took my arm and led me from the church.

Just as we stepped out into the kind of heat that makes me gasp someone must have taken a photograph of the scene, because the picture appeared on the front of the local paper the next day. The coffin was sloped atop the shoulders of the pallbearers as they carried it down the stairs. I was behind, looking down, my face a mask of perfect misery. When I think of the funeral, it is not the sound of sobbing echoing off the church walls or the desolate graveyard among the paddocks or the old ladies bingeing on cakes afterwards that first comes to mind, it is that photograph. Of all the photographs I have ever seen of myself, it is the most honest and shocking.

Soon after her funeral I visited the church again for a Saturday-night service. As we sat there, a strange unseasonable storm blew up. All the lights went out and tiles slid off the roof and smashed on the concrete below as the wind and rain whipped the building. It was tempting to think of it as some kind of message, but it felt hollow and frightening; if it was a message it was a violent one.

Years later it felt alright to be in the church again, thinking of all the services that had gone on since then diminished the hold of my unhappy memories. The priest was advancing towards the congregation, who filled the back two thirds of the pews. He carried a golden bucket, the same size a toddler would be given for the beach, in which was sunk a golden stick. He took the stick from the bucket and began to shake it over the people sitting in front of us, unleashing a spray of Holy Water. When it came my turn to be blessed I felt two drops on my scalp and two on my hands. Across the aisle from us an old lady had received more than the average share of Holy Water, it shone against her tailored navy trousers and ran down her leg onto the pew. After the priest had moved away she took a tissue from her bag and dabbed at the stain, giggling with the woman sitting next to her. I watched the fibres of the tissue disintegrate against her slacks.

For most of the service I kept my mouth shut and my hands by my sides. The only concession to ritual I engaged in was kneeling at the required time so I wouldn't stand out. I watched the rest of the congregation line along the aisle to receive communion, and their faces after they had gulped down the flat, white tablet. Few people drunk from the chalice which held the wine, I suppose it was due to a fear of communicable diseases.

After the handshake of peace, where Adrian, Natasha's father, gripped my pale, plush hand in his rough, scarred one, it was time to leave. I filed out with everyone else and stood outside the church, waiting for the customary post-service socialising to be done with. Pete, the man with the moustache who had led me from the church at the funeral sidled up, and he and Adrian began to discuss a recent auction of farming goods.

'Picked up a bunch of pitchforks on the cheap,' Pete announced, to which Adrian wheezed with laughter and said, 'Well, they'll come in handy.'

When the lights outside the church clicked off most people finished chatting and moved off towards their cars. Doors slammed and engines started, and soon it was only Pete and Adrian, standing in the middle of the street discussing various farming related topics. I wandered away from them. In the sky a gigantic yellow moon was perfectly framed by the silhouettes of trees on either side of the street. It looked lazy, sagging like a yolk, spilling light down onto the clouds striped beneath it. It was beautiful and I wanted someone there to admire it with me, to point up into the sky and exhale in wonder. I knew I should be wishing Natasha was with me, but the town felt empty of her presence. She was being erased.

Earlier that day I had asked Natasha's mother if I could look at the photo albums that record the last few years of her life. She opened a cupboard and retrieved them, warning me, 'Don't bring them out when anyone else is here. They won't understand all that gothic stuff, all that posing and dramatic stupidity. I will burn these eventually.'

The albums sagged in my hands and my polite enthusiasm fled. I wanted to snatch everything left of hers and preserve it. Our dramatic stupidity was everything. Both of us had yearned to live via our imaginations and emotions without having to pretend allegiance to values we didn't believe in. So we dressed up and took tragically staged photographs, cut our wrists and rubbed blood on our teeth, scribbled in notebooks and laughed loudly at jokes only we understood. We screamed from high windows and antagonised the dull with our outrageous appearance.

Without her I was stuck staring at the moon, trying to resist sentimentality and imagine what the scene would be like if she was there. It upset me that I could not guess.

Roy and Joan

The table was covered with impossible amounts of cake. There were sponges and slices, biscuits and cupcakes and pastries, set out on platters and paper plates. I stared out across this table full of cake thinking of all the raw ingredients of it, the bags of sugar and slabs of butter and mounds of eggs. Thinking about it that way made it seem most unappetising.

I was sitting next to a woman who had been introduced to me as Mrs Shirmer. She had stiffly set brown hair and cat eye glasses and was wearing a decorous woollen suit. She was obviously trying to hide the fact she had no idea who I was, or why I had come to celebrate Roy and Joan's fiftieth wedding anniversary. I was confused about this too. The table was surrounded by groups of women wearing dresses in sensible colours: cream, brown, salmon or bottle green. They all knew one another and had a lot to say about very little.

Joan had a degenerative disease which made her unable to remain still. She walked as if she were waltzing, swooping from side to side, her arms sweeping out without warning. Her speech was interrupted by constant twitching. People deftly moved plates of cakes and vases out of the way as she approached, and when she left the room they spoke in low tones about how her condition had slipped since they last saw her.

It was painful having to remain still and look friendly, so I stood up to inspect the cakes. I was given a paper plate with a Christmas design crawling around the rim and obediently loaded it with a slice of cake, a marshmallow biscuit and a caramel slice. I ate the cake as I walked outside and set the plate down on a table, where the slice and marshmallow immediately began to melt in the sun. I left them there, unable to consume any more sugar.

The garden was set up with lawn chairs and umbrellas, and I walked past them to the shed at the back to pat the dog tied up there. It was a Pomeranian with a small, crushable skull, goggle eyes and an unpleasant smelling mouth that housed a lick-eager tongue. It had looped its lead around the wheel of the truck parked nearby. When I sat on the ground cross-legged the wheel was the same height as me, and I felt wonderfully safe and reprieved hiding behind it. The dog pawed and panted at my side, frustrated by its inability to untangle the rope. When I tired of patting it I stood up and slipped out the back gate.

I looked both ways, towards the roundabout on one side and the church on the other. All was hot and still, the treetops did not move, the corrugated iron fence oozed hazy heat into the air. I wanted to sit against the fence until another hour passed and it was time to go. I could picture the scene in the kitchen well, dominated by the old ladies. I tried to remember some of their names: Agnes (don't tell her anything too specific, she's a gossip), Mary (lives next door, likes to bet on the horses, used to work on the telephone exchange in Albury, stays up late), Beryl (one of those small, neat old ladies who wear tailored pantsuits and move swiftly around kitchens). I could have made trading cards out of them, they were such a set. When I left the room Mrs Shirmer was discussing the boarders she had taken into her house after her husband died. I could imagine how the conversation would have progressed, rolling along at a sedate pace, requiring nods and clucks of interest or sympathy.

Back inside they'd been wondering where I'd been, and I said something about stretching my legs. The group in the kitchen had thinned out a bit, and I found a position against the bench, where Trevor was holding one of his sons by the arms to stop him attempting to climb up on his shoulders for a piggy back.

'Did you hear Dot?' he asked. 'Don't take any notice of her.'

'No, why?'

'As you walked inside she was saying, "I hate those girls with hair hanging over their faces."'

I flicked back the two licks of cherry red hair that framed my cheeks and assured Trevor that no harm had been done. The idea that someone might be bothered by my hairstyle was amusing. It took me back to high school where the year coordinator provided me with a daily supply of bobby pins to tie back my fringe, which I preferred to hang over my eyes to avoid making eye contact with anyone. Trevor seemed to need assurance that I was not upset, it had obviously been bothering him. I turned to the urn and the sink and prepared a cup of instant coffee painfully slowly in order to sponge up as much time as possible. As I stood there people began to gather in the kitchen for the cake and the singing of 'For They are Jolly Good Fellows'. I found myself positioned uncomfortably close to Roy and Joan, who stood posing for photographs, grasping a knife above the icing 'Congratulations'. I tried to duck behind the fridge while the photographs were being taken, feeling like an impostor.

After the cake had been divided up by a gang of old ladies I was given the task of distributing paper napkins. I made sure to offer Dot a napkin, although she declined as she was not having any cake. I had been hoping for my hair to flop down over my face at close range and further distress her. With all the napkins gone I went back to the kitchen, where I taunted Trevor's son with the threat that he had to eat the avocado dip.

'NO! Yuck!' he shrieked in delight. I told him that it was delicious, and said that when he was an adult he would find such things very tasty. He looked horrified by the idea. His little sister, a tiny blonde girl with a protruding belly, announced that she was going to tell me which of the party foods she liked. I sat against the cupboards, while she circled the table, chanting:

'Would eat that, would eat that, wouldn't eat that, would eat that.'

After she finished I asked her to show me the best thing on the table, and she thought very seriously before pointing to the 'Congratulations' cake.

'But only the icing,' she said, dragging her finger through the top of the cake.

'Don't do that,' I said. 'You have to take it from the side where people won't notice. See, here,' I said, pointing to a hidden part of the cake. This advice immediately won her over, she looked pleased that an adult was condoning such behaviour. When she finished licking icing off her fingers she came to stand beside me and tried to open the cupboard that I was sitting against.

'Are you trying to catch them?' I asked.

'Catch them?' She looked confused.

'The cups. When you shut the cupboard door they come to life. They're actually having a party in there as well, like we are out here, but when someone opens the door they stand still, so no one catches them. Let's see if we can catch them at it,' I said, slyly opening the cupboard door.

We continued opening and shutting the cupboard for a few minutes, until Natasha's mother came to fetch me. It was time to go. I said goodbye to Joan and Roy, and Trevor, and a more general goodbye to everyone else. I waved to the little girl, and as I walked out into the front garden I heard her scream, 'The cups are having a party!' and an old lady replying, 'That's nice dear.'

Dawn and Vern

'Talk to them, say "Good geesies, that's my geese, good geese."' Vern advanced across the garden, ducking underneath the trees, towards the unwieldy birds. We'd come outside to see the geese, releasing me from the kitchen where I had just consumed a hot cross bun and a piece of chocolate sponge cake. They gurgled together in my stomach, mixing with the tea I didn't usually drink but felt too polite to refuse.

Dawn explained how the tea in England tastes different, which she supposed was due to the different minerals in the water. She also explained how the supermarket in town reduces the chocolate sponge cakes at certain times, and how these cakes keep well in the freezer.

'This is one of Vernies',' she said, indicating the crumbling spiral of cream and chocolate. Vern lived in town, so it was less of a hassle for him to be there at cake reducing time. Dawn's property was further out, it had taken five minutes just to navigate the long, pot-holed driveway.

When we arrived Dawn and Vern were sitting in the sunroom watching *King of Kings*, a movie about the life of Jesus. It was reaching the end and Dawn explained how she thought the final image was very powerful, Christ's shadow lengthening into a cross as he walks along a beach. I thought how strange it would be to act the part of Jesus, but kept my thoughts to myself. 'It was *The Ten Commandments* last year,' she said, referring to the Easter Saturday television programming. I remembered a year before I had watched all four hours of it at my mother's house in Annandale, written a list of my favourite quotes from the film, and made heart-shaped biscuits. I was upset for some reason, and a tear fell onto the baking tray and sizzled as it made contact with the metal. I felt very removed from that day now, being here in Dawn's house, many hours and kilometres away.

The sunroom was cosy and colourful, filled with plants in hanging baskets and macramé pot holders.

'Barry says he needs a machete to get through to the bathroom,' Dawn said. Barry was her son. I noticed the bathroom was marked with a wooden sign in the shape of a duck. Butterflies and deer and gnomes were clustered on the tops of bookcases and cabinets. I stood to admire four plant cuttings growing in glass bulbs. Inside the bulbs their roots spread through the water like spider webs, and I commented how they looked like paperweights.

'Dawn is a very artistic and creative lady,' said Vern, proudly. They were obviously besotted with one another, although they took pains to specify that they were just friends.

'Vern has his own room here,' said Dawn, 'for when he stays. It's good to have company.' Through a doorway off the kitchen I glimpsed a couple of sturdy chairs with lace antimacassars draped over their plump arms, and a spoon collection neatly arranged in a purpose-built cabinet. I longed to explore the house, so often in old country houses the living room is kept like a museum display, most decidedly un-living. I wanted to turn on the light in there and expose everything.

Instead I stood with Vern, admiring the geese. They waddled away from me with slaps of their webbed feet and I appreciated their fine, wide bodies, neat orange beaks and bead-black eyes. Vern carried out a sprinkler and set it up near where the geese were clucking and wandering, telling me they liked to stand underneath the droplets of water. Then he took me on a tour of the garden so the geese could play, they were regarding me suspiciously and nervously and ignoring their sprinkler.

Vern drew back the leaves of a vine and tenderly revealed the tiny cucumbers growing underneath. He showed me the wax plant recuperating in half a plastic drum which once held weed killer, the crossbone warning still visible on the side of it. He greeted a cockatoo in a cage and proudly displayed the wishing well, the rusting swing set, Dawn's collection of begonias. We stood at the gate and looked out at the patchwork fields stretching out to the horizon, where I could see Barry's tractor gliding along. Vern said how proud Dawn and Eric (her late husband) must have been to stand at the gate and look over their farm, and I thought of this image as a black and white photograph.

To explore we had to do a lot of ducking, branches of different trees reached out to one another to form an obstacle course. At one of the corners of the garden we stopped to admire a group of telegraph-pole straight trunks. They were warm from the sun and sprouted soft, felty leaves. He told me that these trees were native to China. Vern seemed very proud of Dawn's garden.

He showed me the old metal milk cans lying on their sides underneath the oleander, telling me that he and Dawn had cleaned them up and were going to see if they were worth something.

'Antique shops like this old-time farm stuff,' he said. I thought how strange it would be to have objects from your past suddenly viewed as antique, items you regarded as commonplace desirable to people as relics of a rustic era.

Before we left I asked to see the chickens. Dawn cleared away the tea things and pulled a John Deere cap over her hair. It looked strange in conjunction with her dark, poppy-patterned polyester dress. It was the type of dress I would select from a rack at an op shop. This fact made me feel immediately comfortable, as if Dawn and I were friends, although I had met her only twice before and she was almost fifty years older than me. I knew she had been close to Natasha and I liked the feeling that Dawn and I had a connection too.

She put on a pair of dark glasses and collected a bucket of food scraps from outside the back door.

'Chickies!' she carolled, as she walked across to the sheds. 'Chick-chick-chickies!' She was so matter of fact, calling to her chickens, that it made me wish I lived in the country and could stride around with buckets of slops, calling out nonsense words.

'I wanted hens, but I have at least six roosters,' said Dawn, referring to the most recently hatched bunch of chickens. 'That speckled one always runs out to greet me, so I can't eat him, but I'll have to eat the others.' She explained how she wasn't able to tell for sure which ones were roosters, for they had not yet grown enough. 'My mother used to say that if they're wearing long pants, then they're roosters.' I noticed that the full grown rooster had feathers covering his wrinkled legs and I understood her mother's analogy. They scrabbled for the kitchen scraps, and I felt sorry for the condemned adolescent roosters pecking vigorously at the ground alongside the precious hens.

I was disappointed to leave. Vern was showing me the photographs from his recent overseas visit. He had been on a coach tour of Britain and Europe and had three large albums, with each photo inside labelled in neat but wobbly writing. The photos were not all that interesting but Vern took a great delight in explaining the circumstances in which he had taken each.

'I got off the bus, walked across the street, and just took the photo.'

'I walked up to the gate and took the photo.'

'I thought it looked interesting, so I got out my camera, and took the photo.'

I thought of how, in the garden, I had picked a small spider off Vern's collar. It was scampering towards his neck, and I quickly apprehended it by picking up the stream of thread issuing out behind it, and transferred it to one of Dawn's plants. It was a strange, almost tender action, and Vern had stood still, waiting for me to tell him it was gone.

Yabbies

The cousins cast out lines of black cotton with sections of meat tied to the ends. The meat bulged out between the loops, like when you wrap thread around your finger to turn it purple and bloodless. They hovered at the edge of the murky dam water, watching the strings for movement.

I was sitting in the ute, not wanting to risk burning my face or neck in the startling sun. I had declined participating in the yabby catching adventure, although I was curious, never having seen a yabby. I didn't even know what they looked like, I pictured a large, lobster-like creature, segmented and armoured in a tough, brown shell.

There were four dams on the property and we drove to each in turn. I sat in the middle of the front seat, beside Aunt Chris and Adrian, who jammed the gearstick back and forth and into my thigh, while apologising. 'Could be misinterpreted,' he said drily. I entertained him by speculating the many times that country lads had changed gears with the purpose of covert groping. Aunt Chris was silent during this conversation, perhaps disapproving. She had a fabric hat strapped around her head, so her face seemed to poke up like the polleny centre of a flower, and she grasped her camera on her lap. The camera bothered me, it was too expectant. It stood for the hope that memorable moments were about to occur and I didn't feel right being a part of them.

The kids and Uncle Kev had to ride in the tray of the ute with various pieces of greasy machinery. The interior was covered in dust and grease and on the floor of the passenger seat was a collection of obscure tools. As I sat sheltering from the sun I picked out what looked like a giant pair of pincers from the pile. They were as big as my face, and when you squeezed the two sections of the handle the pincer-jaws clamped together. I jumped down from the car and performed a pantomime of extracting one of my teeth, for the benefit of the cousins. They laughed at my joke, seemingly wholeheartedly.

It was difficult to know how to act, being a poor replacement for their favourite cousin. My presence made Natasha's death even more apparent. We had many similarities and so perhaps if the cousins blurred their eyes a little they could pretend that I was her, rather than a stranger. It was obvious, though. I was awkward and shy and unable to be like Natasha, who chattered and exclaimed and laughed all in a rush. She had known her cousins since they were babies, there was no way I could approximate anything like her level of intimacy with them. I felt like an understudy who did not know her lines.

We were not lucky at the first dam and drove through various paddocks to try the next one. Adrian paused the ute in front of the gates and Uncle Kev eagerly leapt out of the back to open them at every stop. Sometimes he collided with Adrian, who automatically opened the door and swung out of his seat to open the gate.

At the next dam we were more successful. Adrian flung out circular traps made of wire and hessian with a section of meat attached to the centre of them, and it was when checking one of these that excited yells announced the catch. I picked up one of the yabbies, squeezing behind its claws so it couldn't bite me and examined its brown-green shell with red joints, thick tail, and legs that scrabbled in the air uselessly. After inspecting it I threw it back into the water, muttering 'poor bugger'. When all the traps had been checked and the yabbies transferred to a plastic bucket I watched them scrabbling, fighting each other in frustration. I carefully lifted one out and the rest followed, clamped together in a string, like chain links. I felt sorry for them, and after a few minutes conspired with the girls to let them go. We inclined the bucket towards the water line and encouraged the creatures to crawl back into the dam. In the end we had to tip the whole jumbled mass of them in, but when they made contact with the water they untangled and disappeared into the safety of the mud.

With the yabbying over we drove out to see the lambs again. Adrian and I had gone to check on them the day before. The lambs wobbled around on uncertain legs. Each broad, woolly sheep was shadowed by a meek, pink face and spindly body. I stared at them through the grimy window as Adrian explained how crows are scavengers, and if they are on the ground instead of in a tree it is a sign that one of the sheep is dead and they are picking over the carcass. We drove to where crows were hopping over the grass, and I expected to draw up next to some horrible, rotting creature, but there was nothing. We drove around the flocks of sheep, making sure all the lambs were lively. Any that persisted in lying down Adrian would antagonise with the car horn, and in that way make them stand up and prove that they had not been stricken.

Today Adrian told us that we might catch them gambolling, it being sunset. He described how they frolic – hopping in the air and racing back and forth. I hoped very much to see them gambolling, but when we arrived at the lamb paddock they were either scared or bothered by our interruption. I looked back at the cousins riding in the back of the ute, their denim knees at my eye level. They were nice kids and I felt sad for them no longer having their favourite cousin to play with. My presence broke their family dynamic, I was polite to the point of being insipid and never sure of what to say. I sighed and turned to watch the paddocks instead.

That night we had a special Easter Sunday dinner. On my floral plate was heaped a selection of boiled vegetables. I held a cousin's hand in my right hand and Uncle Kev's in my left as he said a short prayer, thanking the Lord for what we were about to receive. I didn't feel much like eating dinner, mostly because of the taste 'sensation' I had been enjoying earlier in the afternoon in another attempt at slapstick. Potato chips and Easter eggs together left me feeling very queasy.

During the meal I tried to remain chewing so I did not feel obligated to talk. Adrian and Uncle Kev carried out a long conversation about synthetic diesel fuel, Adrian explained how the diesel made from canola plants made your car 'smell like a barbeque'. I laughed at this, perhaps too loudly, as no one else seemed to find it all that funny. I pictured giant barbeques flaming past on the highway outside, rolling on huge wheels.

I refused dessert upon sight of the plates of ice cream subsiding into small slices of cheesecake and excused myself from the table. I went back to the spare room where I had been sleeping. On the way I passed Natasha's room, still with her pictures on the wall and her things on the desk. This was the place in the house where I felt the strongest sense of her, it bulged out the door and lassoed me as I passed.

Stepping inside I felt as if she were watching me and I wanted to ask her if I was doing the right thing. I came to this house because I missed her, but more than that I missed her so much that I wished I could be her, that I could step into her place for a while and it would be like she had come back to life. This didn't work. I just redoubled the feeling of her absence and my inability to make up for it. Her ghost was both everywhere and just out of reach and any question I had for her disappeared into empty air.

I went back to the spare room and began packing my bags for my departure the next day. I knew that looking for Natasha in this house or this town would not give me what I wanted. I wanted her back and I could never have that. There was only one thing that came close. Instead of seeking her out in the world around me I had to look inside myself and remember how after meeting her it was as if I had woken up, and finally felt alive.

Sometimes, You Just Feel Like Spending Two Days as a Rabbit

0 Hours. We don't need Mastercard ads, World No Pants Day or inspirational books by Sark to remind us we can do anything we want. All we need is seventy dollars and a guarantee that we won't try to launder the suits ourselves. *Cheers, have fun, they're due back 10 am Friday.*

The Ladies Only seat outside St Paul's is our meeting place. We imagine how funny it would be to give out infringement notices to men who sit there, but for the most part they're winos who are too pickled to have a sense of humour.

I wait on the wino seat until Steph walks purposefully from Flinders Street station, head down, ignoring the stares from loitering teenage goths and tourists waiting for trams.

She demands I change immediately. I feel reluctant to exchange the op art dress I've freshly purchased from Frankston Savers for the frivolous contents of the plastic bag she has thrust at me, but I don't protest. I follow Steph back into the station and she waits as I struggle in a toilet cubicle, trying to avoid having any of my things come in contact with the damp floor.

The suit includes a shapeless furry sack for a body, a bonnet-style headpiece with floppy pink and white ears and big flaps that cover my shoes. It's baggy and the underside of the fabric scratches; it's a feeling I remember from school plays, sweating and itching inside cheap fabric.

I can't check my reflection properly in the mirrors because they're distorted like the walls of a funhouse. My head zooms from a pea to a balloon. What possible reason is there for this? Surely it doesn't prevent drug use, or crime, or any other nasty thing that might go on in a train station toilet. It just makes it hard for women to check if bits of nori are clinging to their teeth or if their heads have remained the right shape.

Instead of a mirror, I use the faces of the people we pass in the street. Some giggle, some stare, others catch a glimpse then look quickly away in case we try to involve them somehow.

Our first stop is the Golden Tower diner with the flashing lights and the solicitous man at the entrance, inviting people to harden their arteries with potato cakes and Chiko rolls. We order tequila, take a booth and read excerpts from the SCUM manifesto across the lino table.

> *Being completely self-centered and unable to relate to anything outside himself, the male's 'conversation', when not about himself, is an impersonal droning on, removed from anything of human value. Male 'intellectual conversation' is a strained, compulsive attempt to impress the female.*

The room glows yellow and red, I think of pies and tomato sauce. The man behind the counter winks as we pay: *Have a good night.*

As soon as we leave, it starts.

Hey, hey. Easter was four months ago you know.

Our faces stay blank. We decide our only response will be to hop whenever someone in a car honks us.

8 Hours. Standing in the middle of an intersection at Clifton Hill, the air smells of croissants. There's no cars, so no fear of having to hop. We're sick of hopping. Other things we're sick of:

1. Reminders that it isn't Easter.
2. 'Do youse fuck like rabbits?'
3. Guesses which product we're advertising.
4. 'Why are you dressed like that?'
5. People who've taken so many drugs that they don't even notice we look different (e.g. 'Ashtray Face' outside The Lounge).
6. Incoherent yelling from every possible type of vehicle (including streetcleaners).
7. References to Playboy.
8. Jokes about myxomatosis.

We've just spent an hour lying on a patch of lawn, spotting insects in the grass with a torch. It's that dead time of night when there's no one about. The only person we see is a boy holding a tray of unbaked bread rolls inside a Brunswick St bakery, but he doesn't notice us. Probably a good thing, he might have dropped the tray.

In the middle of the intersection it feels like we're inside the mechanism of a watch. The signals tick, the wires overhead gleam. The clicks and twitters thread around us like spiderweb. I feel integrated into the city's secret workings, part of the drains, the tunnels and wires. It is a blissful negation of self. I think how I want this to be my final memory before I die.

12 Hours. Things have deteriorated. The early morning religious programming is demonic, especially on a television set with a green-tinged picture. The hands imploring us to touch the screen for instant healing resemble luminous jellyfish. We switch it off halfway through a song about gentle-Jesus-thank-you-blessed-lamb and sit on the balcony as the dawn cracks over the sky.

We decide we're hungry, but Adam's kitchen is healthy and unpromising. Specifically, there are no warm, fresh jam donuts.

We must have them.

On High St, a group of dark men in bloodstained aprons stand smoking outside a wholesale butchery. They grin at us: *We need rabbits in here.* Their teeth are sharpened to points, their lips are blades, they've come from a room drenched in blood. We put our heads down and increase our pace.

18 Hours. Our suits are getting filthy. It is raining and our paws have become heavy with mud. We're stranded without an umbrella at a tram stop, discussing the morning's significant events:

1. The people in Polyester Books who wanted to film us. *We're looking for an eclectic feel.* Should we have accepted? They were incredulous that we didn't want to be filmed. As if we were doing it for attention!
2. The old lady who excitedly pointed to us as we sat outside Safeway, eating crisps. She dragged a small, ponytailed girl by the wrist, desperately trying to make her react to us. The girl looked indifferent. Human-sized rabbits eating crisps are probably normal to kids, after all they spend their mornings watching cartoons.
3. The billboard of the female newsreader's face with one eye spray-painted black that scared me so much I screamed.

We give up waiting for the rain to stop and trudge back. Ricki Lake's on the telly. Something about hoochie mamas. The ends of our suits are sopping so we rest our paws on the heater and watch steam rise from them.

30 Hours. No one understands. In our world it is just fine to wear rabbit suits and squat at street corners reading quotes from Valerie Solanis. It is fine to eat only crisps and jam donuts washed down with American beer. The citizens of Melbourne have proven their lack of imagination and general idiocy by persisting in substandard jokes about the sex life of rabbits. We are skulking in the dead half of the city, planning our next move.

They are in town for a conference and stray from the flashy innards of the Crown Casino. Not knowing their way around, they trawl the edges of the business district. Tall, nondescript buildings offer them nothing but views of dark foyers, inaccessible behind stilled automatic doors.

We hear their voices approaching, hooting and complaining, arguing whether there is anywhere better to go than the lurid twenty- four hour gambling den across the street. As soon as they catch sight of us, they stop and gasp with laughter.

The loudest of the group, a man with apple red cheeks, begins questioning.

'Why are you dressed like that?'

'Like what?'

'The rabbit suits.'

'I'm sorry, we have no idea what you are talking about.'

'Come on,' apple-face urges. 'Just tell us.' He moves his appeal to me.

'You're quiet, you must be the sensible one. Tell me, why are you dressed like that?'

'I'm sorry, I have no idea what you are talking about. Why are *you* dressed like *that*?'

He looks down at his disheveled smart casual and unfurls the story about the conference and the casino. He and his work colleagues flew in from Brisbane the day before.

'Don't you have things like this in Brisbane? It's normal here.'

One of the women in the group persuades Red-Delicious-face to stop questioning, so she can interrogate us as to the whereabouts of all-night drinking establishments. We shrug and point to the gambling den across the street. It is a rainbow of neon with a gigantic gold coin moving suggestively in and out under the word LUCK.

'Come and drink with us!' they implore.

'No thanks.'

'Come on.'

'No.'

'Sure?'

'Sure.'

Before they leave they extract cameras from their bags and ask us to pose for photographs. We endure their arms around our shoulders. Flashes spark and leave squares floating over our retinas as we watch the group cross the street. They disappear under the giant coin with production-line efficiency, one after the other.

38 Hours. A speed-addled monkey man is showing us how he collects objects of the same colour in plastic sandwich bags. He scratches under a pile of cassettes, boxer shorts, scraps of paper, towels and flyers, looking for the blue bag. One of us is holding a blue lid. We're not allowed to hold it, it has to go into the blue bag.

I slip out of the room and pad down the hallway, looking for the bathroom. I spend a very, very, very long time in there, relishing the ceramic cool and the lack of colour coding.

48 Hours. The rabbit suit is a fluffy grey puddle on the bathroom tiles. I'm being reborn under the shower, my skin is already forgetting the sweaty, scratchy sack in which it has been entombed for the last two days.

The suits are going back to the shop. We weren't successful, but it wasn't our fault.

No understanding, just stupid jokes about rooting or trying to guess what we were advertising. They took offence that we wouldn't let them in on our secret. The only secret was that there was no secret! Sometimes, you just feel like spending two days as a rabbit.

Objects

I Feel Like an Archaeologist of the Recent Past

Second World

They are the kinds of suburbs I would never visit otherwise. Names I associate with other people's aunts, that retain a mysterious aura because I know nothing of them: Chester Hill, Dee Why, Ingleburn. Each is a code for a different experience of suburban life that I can only guess at. I feel like an explorer as I consult my hand drawn maps and notice the details that make these places distinct. These distinctions come with the arrangement of the streets and the architecture of the toilet blocks and the pinkness of the finger bun icing in bakery displays. For missions into the suburbs I dress down. Part of it is not wanting to draw attention to myself in an unfamiliar place, like wearing respectful attire for a cousin's wedding. Also I enjoy the idea of going undercover, of shaking off my usual self for a while. Once I leave my local area I am gloriously anonymous; I won't be recognised and I will recognise no one.

I like how easy it is to feel transformed by travelling to a new suburb. From the train window I watch a procession of backyards flicker past, their Hills Hoists, rusting cars and scattered toys. There is a feeling of accumulation as I pass house after house, of life upon life and all the objects this entails. The red roofs stretch out in all directions and I know it is these houses that jettison the objects I am going in search of.

If the suburbs are unknown, the op shops are familiar. I recognise the motley appearance of the stock, the different sections, the common objects, the types of shoppers and what they talk about, the easy listening radio soundtrack, the colour coded price tags and the door to the secret back room. Once I enter the shop the specific details of the suburb outside recede and I am absorbed by things, as if I have walked into a kind of meta-house where everything people usually keep hidden is out on display. Wardrobes have burst open, kitchen cupboards have been unpacked and I can inspect and touch and take away anything that interests me. Once I have bought something, even if it is merely a pamphlet of cake recipes, I feel as if I have laid anchor in the unfamiliar place I've chosen for my mission. I am a tourist and my souvenir gives me the right to speak on the suburb's behalf. I imagine myself reporting back to a central authority:

'There were dozens of trophies in the bakery window. The houses had the neat, self-contained look of handmade chocolates. I imagine the biggest crime problem would be letterbox vandalism. Every doormat says welcome. In the primary school the kids are bragging about being descended from convicts. No one would have record players anymore, only neat mini CD players and iPods. It is not a place I can imagine hearing the Psychedelic Furs.'

I feel conspicuous walking back to the station with a Psychedelic Furs LP, as obvious as if I'm riding a velocipede. My report would continue: 'I'm easily pleased – I visited between trains and took away a mass-produced pop album from the 80s that cost one dollar.'

To many this must seem like a grubby, marginal activity, all the finger-sticky train railings and crumpled lists of addresses and gold coin purchases. Visits to suburbs where no one travels without a practical reason in order to search through rooms of discarded household objects and come away with a few insignificant things.

As insignificant as it may seem, for me it is essential. In my continued visits to op shops I feel like I am connecting with something that is central to the way I understand the world. I feel like an archaeologist of the recent past, building a history of the world from what it has abandoned. This world often seems impossibly vast, it spreads out in never-ending chains that move further away from my grasp the more I contemplate them. All the people in it and all the things these people own and where these things came from and how they were made. So, rather than try and understand things from the top down, I try and work from the bottom up.

I look at my op shop belongings and think how if I had not been in particular places at particular times I would not have these particular things. Because I acquired them by chance I often wonder how they could be different. If, for example, I had gone to all the op shops I've ever been to just one day later, how much of what I now own would be the same, and what kinds of different things might I have? How would this make my life different? An exchange occurs between me and my objects, I rescue them and they give me guidance. As if in going to op shops I am playing a game in which I need to collect particular clues to know how to proceed. When I haven't been to one for even a couple of weeks I feel restless, thinking of all the things that might be out there and might influence my life in unexpected ways. This is how I think of the 'opportunity' that floats behind their name, that by shopping there I give myself up to chance.

Chance was how I discovered op shops in the first place. It was the early 1990s and most Saturday mornings I escorted my sister from our home in Turramurra to Surry Hills for choir practice. I was instructed to on no account leave the building and wander – it was unsafe. Drug addicts, perverts, maniacs and murderers roamed the streets.

As soon as the choir warble started I was out the door. Sometimes I'd go no further than the newsagent to buy music magazines, but other times I'd wander around Surry Hills, leaving a mental trail of breadcrumbs to retrace my steps. I was in search of interesting things in the badlands. It was on one of these wanders I discovered the St Vincent de Paul on Cleveland St and this is the first time I remember noticing an op shop. There were none in the area I lived although I knew what they were from derogatory comments. The op shop contained the lowest order of things and was the most embarrassing place one's parents could shop.

At thirteen years old I felt a particular disappointment from the months of saving, followed by the purchase and domestication of a new object. Once I owned it another desire would quickly replace it, fashions would change and I'd feel back at the start of a frustrating cycle.

The op shop was different, an explosion of cheap, miscellaneous things. I was still enough of a child to regard objects as mysterious and fluid in identity. Without being told what something was by labels and logos and packaging, these objects were mine to define. It was far from the measured experience of shopping malls where I felt uncomfortable and powerless in front of inaccessibly expensive products.

I liked the personal nature of op shopping, going through people's things. I'd always been interested in other people's houses and was a terrible snoop. I peeked into bathroom cabinets and desk drawers and paid special attention to the framed portraits and ornamental plates my friends' parents displayed in their lounge rooms. When they left the room I would poke my nose into the cupboards but make sure I was sitting angelically by the time they returned. I was never caught in the act and shamed into believing this was an unacceptable thing to do. I would not have been convinced by this argument anyway, because it seemed like the easiest way to learn about people was through their things. In the op shop I had found a place I could snoop to my hearts content.

It was also a way I could soak up experiences. My new obsession with music saw me idolising people who seemed so alive with eccentricity, living under the spotlight scrutiny of the music press. I was addicted to reading the *NME* and *Melody Maker* and absorbed the articles about the British bands, new and old, they fetishised: The Smiths, Suede, Huggy Bear, Siouxsie and the Banshees. I quickly worked out one thing they all had in common – their clothes were obviously secondhand. Maybe this was the magic thing that sparked their allure.

Secondhand clothes gave me a way to show that I wasn't like other people by snubbing my nose at fashion. I felt far more confident wearing these clothes, as if I had adopted some of the life they had before I bought them. I spent a lot of time romanticising about who might have owned them previously and embroidering complex stories about their origins. I'd always been like this. The life I lived inside my mind seemed far more real to me than the everyday world of school and my imagination could be so relentless I sometimes felt scared of it. School taught me long division and capital cities but not how to cope with being stuck inside my head.

I realised that it was easier to deal with my wayward imagination if I anchored it to things and the mysterious pasts of secondhand objects opened a space for my thoughts to cavort. Buying from op shops made me feel I was using the world around me for my own purposes rather than conforming to expectations I felt remote from, the new appliances and shiny cars and professional futures of private school kids. I started to rummage.

By the end of the 1990s I was so obsessed with op shopping that I needed to make something more of my experiences with them. I decided to visit every St Vincent de Paul op shop in Sydney and document what I found. I made a zine, *Vinnies*, from my findings. Although ostensibly the focus, the making of the guidebook was secondary. I felt I needed to test my obsession; at the end of my exploration would I have this out of my system?

If anything, it gave it structure. Now I had explored the suburbs, I felt as if the whole network had come alive. I think of them out there and the map of Sydney lights up with possibility. Every new excursion feels like a part of a never ending search. This search continues at night, in my dreams:

I find a men's shirt with a pattern of coffee trees and tiny men picking the beans. I recognise the type of shirt, made out of soft poly-cotton and shaped for a tall, slim body. It reminds me of a particular melamine plate I liked as a child and I know that this is the perfect item of clothing. I could use it as a love letter by giving it as a present.

There was an aquarium shaped like a flying saucer in sunflower yellow that gave me a vertiginous feeling when I looked into it, like putting on a pair of thick bifocals.

I had arms full of fabulous dresses but I couldn't find the counter. I could find no way to buy the dresses but couldn't leave without paying for them. I woke up before I found the counter.

It's my version of an erotic dream, searching for perfect objects among clutter. In the best dreams I find them and feel deliriously satisfied. The pursuit of these objects is my focus, in both my dreams and the waking life they reflect.

What do these perfect objects do? They shock me, like the sudden resurfacing of a forgotten memory. All of a sudden I can't imagine my life without them and I feel like they have always been a part of me. But they are also strange because they can never be wholly mine. They always retain some of the mystery of their previous life, no matter how deeply I have assimilated them. And because I go in search of them without knowing what they are my collection can never be complete. The thought of more of these objects out there, remaining undiscovered unless I go looking for them, puts me back on the train.

Once out of Rockdale station I accelerate in the direction of the Salvos. The op shop is like a magnet, I feel myself drawn to its dusty heart. I know little about this suburb otherwise. The shoe repair stores and post offices and banks might as well be ornamental. They belong to day-to-day life whereas all the secondhand stuff belongs to what lies behind it.

Walking inside, the combined amnesia of the objects in the store surges to greet me. Who used to own these things? Why did they give them away? Do they ever think of them now? Do they have photographs with these things in the background? Did they imagine what would happen to them? Everything in here is in a kind of purgatory, in between waste and usefulness, waiting for rescue. I imagine that in the alleyway behind the shop a skip bin bulges with the memories discarded from these objects. These memories leak out into the drains and dissolve in the water supply and come back to people in dreams.

I abandon myself to the racks and shelves, running my eyes over the clothes and pulling out appealing fabrics. Dust builds up on my fingers from flipping through the records and picking up crockery and examining trinkets. I search through every section like I am ransacking a house. Within this activity, I myself feel like an amnesiac. My usual thoughts recede and stories rush through me, impression after impression:

The old-man cardigans, all the same size, could only be chilly living rooms and cups of tea made by the carer. The piles of VHS movies are the corollary to the discarded foam shells of DVD players on rubbish night, the set of pale yellow Johnson Bros. teacups are the back of the kitchen cupboard and all that lurks behind the things we use every day.

I pick up a metal ice bucket in the shape of a pear. It is orange, the colour I imagine infused the 70s. The world was a solid orange until an earthquake shattered it into kitchen utensils, typewriters, recipe boxes and poufs, the shards of which can be collected from op shops all around the city. The ice bucket goes under my arm immediately. I have an apple-shaped ice bucket at home for it to marry.

If there is nothing to hurry me up, I have endless patience. I will look through everything down to the last button.

Sitting cross-legged on the floor my eyes are level with piles of magazines. They are so tightly packed that the only way I can search through them is by pulling out a bundle and relocating it to my lap. I flick through the fishing magazines and knitting patterns and guides to wax museums and celebrity gossip from five years ago and booklets of piano exercises. I pause on a copy of *Gourmet* magazine from 1963 and read 'You Asked For It', the letters page:

> *Q. One of my favourite dishes is Chinese fried rice, a subject on which my cookbooks are silent. I would like to have a recipe for it and I wonder if certain utensils are necessary.*
>
> *RICHARD H. KRUSCHKA*
> *WEST CHESTER, PENNSYLVANIA*

Clocks wind backwards, the calendar flips, the globe turns and I'm plunged into Richard H. Kruschka's kitchen as he heats two tablespoons of peanut oil in a frying pan.

I add the magazine to my 'keep' pile. This now includes the pear-shaped ice bucket, a pair of pale pink slippers with a fluffy rosette on the toe (file alongside Valium/boxed chocolates/*Bold and the Beautiful*/mid-afternoon) and a postcard of a couple examining a cannon in Penang, her in a nautical striped smock, him in tiny red shorts with a clunky SLR slung over his shoulder. On the back, in blue biro script:

> *Hello Everyone, Really enjoying my holiday in Penang.*

The rest of the card blank.

At the bottom of my pile is a photo album with a picture of Sydney on the front. It is old enough for there to be no Centrepoint tower and this makes the city look naïve, like a freshly planted tree. The back cover is a mirror image of the front and when I open it out flat the covers form a butterfly with the Opera House at the centre of the spine.

The effect is Sydney duplicated, with Harbour Bridges arching off in different directions. The back cover Sydney is inverted, and I imagine that this other Sydney acts as a repository of all the objects in my pile. Here the city skyscrapers are vast storehouses for the debris of twentieth century life.

They contain rooms of ice buckets and pamphlets from defunct airlines and ceramic bluebirds and grey overalls with names embroidered on the chest and cheese plates and genie bottles and foolscap ledgers. This world operates on waste and memory and is the world of the op shop.

Departing with Richard H. Kruschka and the rest of my chosen objects I feel ebullient. On the train I take them out and examine them closely, one by one. It is a simple sort of magic that never fails to inspire me: I came across these things by chance and now they are mine. Each time I rescue an object the feeling of salvation extends to myself. I am all-powerful in the realm of these things, I have chosen them and their fate now lies with me.

Bring your desires down to your means! runs through my head as I struggle home after yet another mission a week later. Making up slogans for my army of one distracts me from my aching arms. Plastic bags with strangely bulging contents dangle from them and I'm balancing a giant wooden fork and spoon in the crook of my left elbow. This makes my shadow a strange shape against the pavement and makes people who pass me break into smiles.

Open the dictionary at 'inessential' and here's a list of my purchases: a toilet roll doll with a froofy pink skirt, a set of turtle-shaped coasters picturing the Golden Gate Bridge and a play set of Noah's Ark 'containing Noah and his family, the Ark, domestic animals, wild animals, trees, supplies'.

There is something luxurious in this uselessness, a celebration of whimsy and surplus that could get me down – I live in a world where *this* is mass produced? – if I didn't feel that I'm at least saving these things from landfill. The possible injustices of their production feel distant by the time they make it to the op shop.

Yes, the giant fork and spoon were once part of a tree, but my thoughts are stuck to an image of them hanging in a lounge room against nicotine yellow wallpaper, having been on the wall so long that they seem a part of it. Then, after thirty years, someone decides it is time to redecorate. The fork and spoon are sent to the op shop and hung in the front window and this is where I find them.

My heart leapt as soon as I spied them. After passing up other giant forks and spoons in previous years, I decided that now these items had to enter my life. Whatever erroneous perception of Polynesian culture they were based on was remote to my desire. How could I pass up a fork and spoon the same length as my arms? I asked the lady working there to get them out for me. She unlocked the little gate that lead to the windows, moved picture frames and gingerly stepped onto a raised platform to reach them. When I apologised she said, 'People think it's such a big hassle for me to get things out of the window, but that's what they're there for. People often don't notice something until it's in the window. They often don't know how to put things together.'

The giant fork and spoon were put together with a selection of 7" records including 'My Way' by Frank Sinatra, some wooden horses, a dinner set patterned with tulips, amber glass decanters and mannequins in twin sets. Their putting together seemed to be guided by this recipe: take the contents of suburban homes, shake them up, label them with 'as is' price tags.

'Squeaks $1' – a small plastic mouse.

'Counted. One Piece Missing. $2' – a jigsaw puzzle.

'$3 Bag of Knobs' – I smirked and unzipped a toiletries bag to reveal a collection of wooden doorknobs.

Behind the 'STAFF ONLY' sign the sorting rooms contain taxonomists pondering where the pieces fit. They order the world of unwanted objects into sensible categories. They pick out the fridge magnets from the banana slicers, they separate the jigsaw puzzles from the electric can openers, and decide prices for objects of questionable value.

Noah's Ark, for example, was three dollars. *ONLY DANIEL'S* is messily scrawled over it in black marker, including the surprisingly correct apostrophe, a possessiveness that once seemed so crucial, long dissipated. The sides were taped down so there was no way to get in. I shook it and wondered, listening to the rattle, whether there was one of every animal, domestic and wild, inside and decided it was worth the gamble.

At home I release them. The animals are malformed and crazy in the way of all 'Made in China' plastic animals. They are strange creatures: leopards with giant eyes, pale pink hares in startled poses, monkeys with arms like drowning swimmers, crocodiles the colour of chocolate, a baboon the same size as a piglet with a stegosaurus ridge down its back from the mould it was cast in.

Weird animals abound in op shops. A mouse dressed in orange overalls holding a swag strides across the linen fibres of a tea towel, a complacent cat guards an ashtray, penguins the shape of milk bottles pattern a T-shirt. They are extinct creatures, unable to adapt to the modern world, and this is where they end up.

My all-time favourite weird animal is The Elephant. People shudder when I pluck him from my mantelpiece to show them. About the size of newborn baby, The Elephant has other disturbingly infantile qualities like flesh-pink plastic skin moulded into soft wrinkles and a chubby-cheeked expression of joy. The Elephant is a test case for how far a representation of an animal can stray while still being identified as that animal. The ears are wrong, the trunk is wrong, the head is wrong, the body is wrong, the eyes are wrong, the tusks are non-existent. He is obviously male but for unclear reasons as his smooth, plastic underside is devoid of any clues. All of this somehow adds up to an elephant and what's more, he squeaks if you squeeze him.

The Elephant is from a country op shop, a place long regarded as containing multitudes of fascinating things untouched by local residents who have not caught on to ironic, retro style. This state of affairs is now generally ruined when someone in town discovers Ebay. I imagine the elephant would have been safe regardless, he is not Collectible, not Vintage, not Disneyalia, he is nothing but strange and perfect for me.

I discovered The Elephant in a crate full of toys, a section of op shops that I usually pass over because the thought of milky, mushed-biscuit toddler hands roaming through them makes me feel nauseous. But I was drawn to his wrinkled snout poking out from the toy pile, I felt my mind whirr at a higher gear and my heart rate increase. At the counter the blue rinsed ladies paused their debate about what to dress the mannequin in to remark, 'Isn't he cute?' and I said, 'I'm not sure, but there's *something* about him.'

They charged me two dollars, a small price to pay for the leisure of endless contemplation. He was obviously a toy and meant to be cute but whoever designed him went too far with the signifiers of cute and made something very perplexing. I imagine The Elephant in the hands of a child, the accessory to games, perhaps a fragment of someone's memory revived only when they try and remember the toys they used to play with. Now his new life is to sit in my bedroom and disturb my guests.

Op shops are a type of Noah's Ark, filled with a whole menagerie of minor things cast adrift. Endangered species languish and sometimes I feel like saving them just because I feel sorry for them. I examine a pile of cassingles in cardboard sleeves that enclose 1989 in a time capsule. For a moment I remember watching *Video Hits* on weekend mornings as a child, when music seemed such a glossy and remote thing and pop stars belonged to the same order as cartoons. All these awful songs: 'Toy Soldiers' by Martika, 'Better' by the Screaming Jets, 'Infinity' by Guru Josh. I want cassingles, I don't want cassingles. I think how one day there will be none left, and the idea of them will be as foreign to kids as my grandmother's stories of washing clothes in a copper. It makes me realise the future does not need cassingles. I leave them on the shelf for someone who thinks the future *does* need cassingles, or is crocheting wristbands out of cassette tape, or is looking for pass the parcel presents for a 90s party.

The store where I have my cassingles crisis is called 'Second World'. I like this name because it describes the feeling I get from op shopping. Travelling around the network of op shops in a city feels like traversing a world dispersed across the obvious one. The Second World is of basements and attics and cupboards, of things usually hidden. It has a particular climate (dust, easy-listening radio), particular population (the elderly, the poor, the idle, the bargain hunters) and particular life forms (strange animals, obsolete machines).

As well as making up a piece of this world, each shop has its own internal order. Often the deeper you go into a store the more complex and messy it gets. At the back is where the baggy homemade fancy-dress clothes hang and the bed sheets dwell in faded piles. The bric a brac jumbles together and the knitting patterns breed. Underwear still in packets bears old price stickers from Coles New World for 71 cents. I find things like a palm-sized wooden chair with an anodised metal dish in the seat – a miniature commode?

It is a horrible thing and I have to fight with myself to buy it. I feel like I have a responsibility to buy such curious things because of the turmoil they hatch in my mind; like a traumatic event, I feel a need to talk about it to reconcile it.

I expect the lady behind the counter to comment on my purchase, but her only response is to slightly raise one eyebrow. I suppose there's not much you can say about a small model commode with anodised pan or the kind of person who would buy such a thing. At home, no one can decide what this object is intended for. An ashtray? A shot glass? A container for mints? Not knowing is too much for me, I give the commode away to a ten-year-old boy who puts a tealight candle in the pan and calls it 'The Toilet of Death'. For every thing there is a rightful owner.

Perplexing objects are far outnumbered by redundant ones. When I started going to op shops the technological relics for sale were the manual typewriters, Super 8 cameras and slide projectors of my parents' time. Now the objects have caught up to my life and I take their abandonment more personally.

I feel sad when I see piles of cheap, plastic 35-mm cameras. I cannot imagine why anyone would buy them or why an op shop would bother putting out a crate of old cameras, but some of them, usually the big warehouse stores, do. I look through a pile of them in the Wollongong Salvos. Their differences are subtle, but with enough scrutiny each seems individual, like a group of schoolgirls in uniform. I think of all the photos that must have been taken with these cameras, the prints stored in albums or shoeboxes, framing people's childhood memories. Knowing this, the cameras now seem as empty and hopeless as skulls. Beside them are equally forlorn items, bulky old mobile phones. I could kit myself out as an anachronism, snapping photos with my 35-mm, talking into my redundant phone, decked out in cummerbunds, a great many of which I find in the necktie section. They are difficult to adapt. Ugly polyester dresses, yes, even men's walking socks (in plentiful supply in op shops) have a use, but not the cummerbund. While dressing like a grandparent has ironic value, dressing like a politician at a function can never be cool. They languish, impervious to revival or adaptation.

I like these things that no one wants. Most of the time I'm not interested in buying them, but it's important that there's a place I can go to be reminded of their existence and reflect upon how and why they ended up in purgatory. Op shops are a kind of fluctuating museum where I go to examine the things that most people no longer feel are necessary. Like white gloves and crock pots and old cardigan patterns with relaxed gents and sprightly ladies on their front covers. These couples look so outdated it is difficult to remember that they were once real people. For all their sprightly poses and healthy flushed cheeks, they get little attention.

New arrivals are always most desirable. When someone appears lugging bags of donations to the counter, everyone looks up, interested. The bags are naturally full of The Good Stuff, that doesn't make it to the shelf because the staff take it for themselves.

I used to think this myself but when I started volunteering at an op shop I realised that many things people donate are on the bad side of useless: ripped tracksuit pants, failed sewing projects, greying singlets, plastic bowls with melted sides. The search I had performed so many times in the stores is mirrored in the sorting rooms as staff pass judgement on what deserves another life.

When I mentioned working in the op shop, people's first response was usually,

‘Wow, you must get the pick of all the stuff.’

Like there is a seam of quality items, held in those back rooms, inaccessible to the shoppers who look over piles of empty Danish cookie tins and dream of better things. It is tempting to imagine the inaccessible areas of op shops full of desirable things kept just out of sight. It intrigued me greatly and this was part of the reason I volunteered. What secret rites went on back there?

It was thrilling to be able to transgress the line between shopper and staff member, as if I had suddenly risen to the lower ranks of royalty. Mostly my jobs were to tidy the racks of clothes and hang new ones out, serve behind the counter, and sort and fold the linen. I struggled and sweated through piles of bedspreads and fitted sheets, sleeping bags and ruffled valances. The dust from all this unwanted bedding triggered my allergies and I had to keep tissues poked into my sleeves ready to capture my sneezes. Bedspreads were the worst – sometimes I felt they were about to get the better of me as I attempted to fold them, that they would consume me like a carnivorous plant while old ladies messed up my freshly folded piles. It was as if the dust alerted these women, triggered a siren in their homes that sent them waddling to the store in the hope of lace curtains.

My unofficial role was to chat to Simon, who worked there full time. This was an important part of the job, especially as Simon seemed like the human equivalent of something rare and wonderful that might be found in an op shop. Every week I'd come in and exclaim over some new object in the cabinet, take it out and fiddle with it. Simon would tell me facts about it gleaned from Yvette, the manager, or one of the customers, or from his own journeys within the covers of obscure library books. More than anyone I know he had a huge capacity for wonder. I knew that no matter how insignificant an object was, he was the only person who would not find it strange that I found it interesting.

So he priced piles of easy-listening records and chatted to the old folk of Dulwich Hill, to whom he was a kind of hero. In the background I sneezed through bags of linen, thinking that if I owed anything to the world, it was this. To struggle with other people's unwanted clothing, to balance all the stories I have made by imagining other people's lives.

Although linen duty could seem penitential, I knew I belonged in the op shop. It felt right to act as a custodian of outmoded things, in a place where people paid attention to detail and found worth in the negligible. It was a system I understood and felt part of. Practically everything I own is secondhand, so I was very at home among the jumble. Wearing my completely secondhand outfits, I imagined that if I stood still enough I'd be mistaken for a mannequin and someone might try to undress me.

Often whole estates were donated. Estates were exciting. The truck rattled to a stop out the front, full of the contents of a recently deceased person's house. The sorting room then filled with boxes and the sweet, musty scent of a stranger's home. One time I was hanging around, talking to Yvette as she unpacked some of these. The box she was looking through had been packed haphazardly, its contents miscellaneous as if whoever had done it had flung in everything within reach. This included a collection of pipes. They were the kind my father used to smoke, with the same tarry hearts and smooth wooden stems.

Also in the box were piles of birthday cards. Naturally such personal things are discarded, but with my love of paper ephemera I could not help reading them first. As Yvette continued to methodically sort through the box, I picked out a handful of the cards. In one, a Valentine's Day card with a cutesy cartoon on the front, the message written inside was a drawing of a pipe with smoke rising from it and three kiss x's underneath.

In all my years of being an op shopper I have never felt much of a sense of the actual people who used to own the objects I look through. It is easy to create characters around objects while knowing there is no way to find out the truth. But here, this was once a complete life. The pipes belonged to a man whose death was perhaps in part due to smoking them, who loved the woman whose unused notepaper and trinkets were all around us. These things were part of the meaningful order of their lives, but once they were sorted through, divided up into trash and shop stock, they lost this order and became merely objects.

The next week, the pipes were for sale in the cabinet for five dollars each.

One of the most common criticisms of op shops comes with a nose-wrinkle of revulsion: that they are full of dead people's things. This has never worried me as I do not believe death is contagious. Op shops themselves are very alive places, full of bustle and fossicking and conversations and potential. If anything, they are about reincarnation rather than death, as objects find new homes and uses.

The more you visit op shops, the more possibilities flower. Things come alive, connections form. To get to this stage you need patience and the ability not to be discouraged by ugliness, excess and grime. With attention to detail you will find your appreciation of objects grows.

You might become like me. In the Men's Shirts section of Bankstown Salvos I found myself examining a label sewn into a shirt collar that read:

JAMES BOND
007
BY PELACO
Luxury Imported Fabric
Terylene/Cotton 15-15½

Smiling at the tiny gun embroidered beside the 007, I realised I have become the kind of person who can be both absorbed and amused by a shirt label. Although it was just a shirt label, it connected to a web of other shirt encounters: buying shirts for men I've had crushes on, my brief shirt and tie and trousers phase at age twenty, being in a country op shop and remarking how there were a lot of small men's shirts and a lady saying, 'they get too fat for 'em when they get old'.

I put the shirt back and moved on to the Ladies Dresses, the floor creaking beneath my step. The clothes section of Bankstown Salvos is upstairs and this makes the activity of searching even more like rummaging through an attic. I have never been in a proper taxidermy-and-dusty-suitcases attic, but I know from books and movies that attics contain secrets, stories and debris, and so are my type of place.

I flipped through the dresses quickly, skimming my eyes over their shoulders. I can usually work over a rack in thirty seconds and assess if there's anything of interest.

This time my jaw dropped and I exhaled hard. I'd found another cloud dress! I checked the label and it was my size! What were the chances?

The original cloud dress is a pink, floor-length, floaty 70s number. At the bottom of the dress are printed fields and trees, which evanesce into the clouds that cover the rest of the dress. It is like wearing a pink sky and its effect is strong; it makes me want to float between rooms at parties. I cannot imagine anyone could have worn the cloud dress sober. It could only be the product of an era of key parties, drink driving and menthol cigarettes, designed to be viewed in a drunken haze.

This dress was the same, but blue!

I never expect to come across duplicates of my dresses, although I know most must have been mass produced. I wonder about the fate of their sisters sometimes. Some must still be hanging in wardrobes, others turned into rags or insulation, others in dress-up boxes.

I scuttled to the change rooms with my prize. The change room doors were covered in notices, all of which I ignored, things like 'Apply to the security officer before entering fitting room'. There was no security officer, the space was empty except for me and a Christian radio station playing a poppy song about the birth of Jesus. The Christian radio background music and the embroidered Bible verses on the walls of op shops are comforting. I feel safe in this environment, connected to yellowing childhood memories of stuffy church halls and Saturday morning fetes. I feel even safer in op shop change rooms, enjoying the momentary pleasure of having my own private compartment.

I twisted the lock on the door, wriggled out of my clothes and into the cloud dress. It fit perfectly. The other dress I chose to try on had puffy sleeves and left me looking strange and misshapen, like an oversized child. Chance rules with op shop dresses. It can be stunning but I have to give up if it doesn't fit. I've tried to squash myself into dresses two sizes too small, in the delusional hope they were donated to the op shop because the wrong size was printed on the tag. I've bought so many too-big dresses with intentions of modifying them but never doing so that I placed a decree upon myself – only buy it if it fits.

Downstairs among the furniture I discovered a set of white suitcases with red satin interiors. They looked so nice when I opened their lids that I wanted to climb in there and rest in mothball-scented luxury. There was a name and address written on the lining in black marker: G. Anderson, 2 Smith St, Merriwa. I tried to imagine what existed now at the address where the suitcases were once anchored, picturing a street of fibro houses in a country town, shimmering under heat haze. I wanted the luggage but there was no way I could carry it back with me on the train, and my scrutiny had alerted others. As I moved away a man rapped on them to test their strength. I didn't look back because I didn't want to see him buying them.

In the middle of the shop was a long table covered in computer monitors, all ugly, grubby grey. It was like a collection of pebbles. As I regarded them, thinking *no one's ever going to buy these*, I noticed two people sitting on a saggy brown couch staring at me. Staff? Shoppers? I moved off self-consciously towards the bric a brac and their eyes followed. Op shops are great places for people with nothing to do. If you're elderly, on the pension, out of work or lonely it's alright to just hang around and stare or strike up conversations. Saggy brown couches are usually provided.

just like walmart!

At the counter I couldn't help telling the guy working there about my good fortune.

'I have the exact same dress, but in pink. What are the chances of finding another one?'

This news pleased him and he said, 'We get all sorts of things in here.' This is the proud boast of the op shop employee – we are the guardians of treasure, the gatekeepers of a tide of stuff that has the potential to contain anything and everything.

'A woman came in looking for a particular cookbook. She used to own it but lost it somehow and now wanted it again. Anyway, I said she should come in regularly and keep an eye on the book section. After a few months, she found another copy there!'

He appeared certain that with a little stamina and patience eventually any desired object would turn up. It made me remember a story in a children's book I used to own. There was a massive flood but a little boy who was safely lodged in an attic (among the redundant objects) was above the water line and able to watch things floating past: elephants, jumping castles, suitcases, trousers. He could fish out things as they passed. This is what I feel like I am doing by op shopping, out of all the random stuff for sale I select the few things that I think could be of use or interest, take them home and add them to my belongings.

'Yes, we get a lot of stuff. My thing is mugs, but I've been instructed not to bring any more home. I have four boxes of them.'

'That's alright, I have three wardrobes of clothes,' I said, leaning conspiratorially over the counter. I understand the inertia of collecting, fixing on particular objects and finding them more and more meaningful, like books without end.

I was holding up the line at the counter with my chatting. The woman behind me tried to speed things up by removing the clothes she wanted to buy from their hangers. I also have a habit of doing this when I'm waiting. Things can take a while at the counter, because much is exchanged beyond money. The customer confesses a collecting habit, or justifies their purchase, or gloats about their good luck. When I worked behind the counter I would often look over the objects people were buying and examine them – isn't this unique/interesting – and they would feel they had made a great discovery. Simon was even better than me at this, every object had *something* significant about it, no matter how negligible. We were the ideal people to work in an op shop because we were so attuned to things. No matter how obscure or ugly an object might be, we liked to think that there was someone for whom it would be perfect.

Do other op shop staff think so closely about things? What did the staff of Gladesville Vinnies think of Natasha and I when we took armloads of velvet and fake fur into the change rooms? We were two black-haired girls dressed in black, excited to be playing dress-ups together. She was my first friend who was as interested in op shops as me and our common aim was to buy the clothes that would make us look like the dangerous women we idolised. Our clothes gave us the power to change identities, to transform ourselves. Better than being famous was the ability to choose between being a starlet or a consumptive maiden or a debonair wastrel, just by changing our clothes. Gladesville Vinnies was particularly good for gloves and our first stop was always the chest of drawers where the accessories were kept, to open one by one the individually labelled compartments: Gloves, Purses, Belts, Haberdashery and Bow-ties. There was a particular pleasure in pulling each drawer open, as we hoped to find a perfect example of any of these lying inside, waiting for us.

Eight years later the same drawers are still being used for these items. I'm here alone, on a solitary north-west op shop mission. This time the drawers hold nothing that stands out and I end up bypassing the clothes altogether because there's a couple frantically going through them looking for 'vintage'. I know this is what they are looking for when one of them pulls out a brown and yellow 70s bedspread from the linen section with a pugilistic look of triumph.

It makes me nervous to have competition. As moralistic as I can get that I'm on a higher plane to the Ebay-ers and retro stall holders, we share a similar value system, looking for the authentic and eccentric. In these situations I have to give myself a motivational talk – let them be. I always find good things and there's no point in being greedy.

Anxiety has ruined the romance of my search, so I devise a game: *With all the desire flooding the shop I will search for the least desirable object.* I go straight to the cassettes and videos and am quickly rewarded with a cassette of *Anne Sullivan Sings Marie's Songs*, produced for the Wyalong Centenary Celebrations, 1894 – 1994. Marie's songs have buoyant, religious titles such as 'He Has Given Us the Wheat'. The cover art is a wonky drawing of a well, the pencil sketch shadow still visible behind the ink, and on the back is printed, 'Welcome Back to Wyalong, G-Day G-Day'. No one would want this, unless in a lottery-winning coincidence a Wyalong local history fanatic happened to be shopping in Gladesville Vinnies.

Op shops can be passionate places. The security of a first-hand shopping environment doesn't exist – you have to grab things straight away or face never seeing them again. You can touch them, carry them around, test them out and spend as long as you want deciding whether you need them or not. I've sometimes been hopelessly fixated on an object that someone else is holding, trying not to let it bother me as I stand in front of the books, too overcome to read the titles. Telling myself that if I don't watch, they will put down the dress or vase or soup pot or tablecloth they are holding so I can snatch it up. This rarely happens, desire makes the air heavy. I always know when I'm holding something someone else wants. I remember once a pale, ponytailed girl looking forlornly at the bright floral shirt I had found, dithering around looking at nothing until I went to the counter to buy it, at which point she fled the store. Hating me, no doubt. In my joy in purchasing it I also felt like a rotter, knowing I had a wardrobe like a 70s boutique and she was probably just discovering life beyond denim.

I like browsing alongside the elderly best, they are rarely interested in the same things as me and I enjoy listening to their conversations. At the next store up the line from Gladesville the ladies behind the counter wistfully discuss how much they wish they could be outside in the sun, rather than being stuck behind the counter. A customer warns them that, despite appearances, 'it's a bit nippy'. They start to talk about how these days kids never go in the sun and are getting deficient in Vitamin D. 'I used to let my kids out in the sun all the time,' says one of the staff members. 'I'd give them sun baths.'

'People these days are too careful,' the customer replies. 'My kids used to get out there and eat dirt, didn't do them any harm.'

Pause. 'Yes, that sun looks nice.' The staff ignore the dirt comment.

As their conversation continues in this vein, I stare into a 1978 calendar tea towel. Does anyone ever check the date by looking at a calendar tea towel? As well as the calendar, the tea towel features a cartoon Australia stippled with landmarks and giant wildlife. A koala hovers atop the Harbour Bridge and a huge black swan links Perth and Kalgoorlie. I stare at the number marking the date of my birth, as if trying to extract some kind of secret about my origins. Perhaps this was used to dry dishes on the day I was born. I know the type of meals that were eaten then from my collection of old cookbooks. I own the type of clothes and aprons people wore while cooking them. I think about collecting a calendar tea towel from every year from then to now. In that way I could be reminded of every day that I've lived and think about it while drying plates that used to be part of other people's dinner sets.

When I find such obvious links to my past – something from 1978, or something my family used to own – I wonder whether my fascination with op shops and secondhand objects is in fact an obsession with my origins. A desire to know the world into which I was born by scrabbling through its debris. All I can know of the world before my birth is fragments and clues and stories, and objects from then help to fill the gaps. Although that time will always be a remote, fantasy place subject to the push and pull of my imagination, I often find it easier to grasp than the present; perhaps this is because I *can* grasp it, in the form of tea towels and Tupperware and melamine ashtrays.

Now there are few 70s relics in op shops and I see my own life and memories reflected in the objects there. Everyday things from the 80s and 90s and more recent years that I have forgotten about and would not have remembered otherwise. I feel that by encountering these objects again, out of context, I have a chance to think about change, both in the world and in me. I put the tea towel over my arm and resolve to use the bus trip home to calculate how many days I have been alive.

Then the couple who annoyed me in Gladesville Vinnies enter the store. They are obviously mining the same strip. The woman pushes past me to get to the clothing and her partner urgently asks the staff, 'Do you have any wedding dresses?' Maybe I misjudged them and they are just desperate to get married. He goes to the fancy dress section with a gasp of delight, thinking that the black jacket with silver details on the shoulders is a real military jacket. I have already examined this corner, so I know that it is actually a poorly constructed prop from a school play, decorated with cardboard and foil.

I decide to wait around for a while after they leave, so I don't have to see them at the next store. I try on a pair of shoes with white fluffy inner soles that I pick out between my thumb and forefinger. Inner soles are awful things and part of me is disgusted that I have made physical contact with them. Another part of me enjoys the intimacy of touching them and imagining what other people would think: my enemies with a picture of me pulling an inner sole out of a dead lady's shoe with the caption, 'She Enjoys This'. Also I like the fact these inner soles are fluffy to give the effect of treading on soft carpet no matter the walking surface. The shoes fit me but I decide not to buy them, knowing that op shop shoes always retain the shape of the foot that wore them before and can never quite be comfortable.

I also decide against the novel that can be read from two directions. At first I think it is an interesting concept. Its identical covers enable the reader to flip the book over and begin reading from the back (now the front) and vice versa. Then I open it and read a sample sentence: *Her womb, once barren, had been filled with his seed.* It goes back on the shelf to join the out of fashion diet books. It is the kind of sentence I live in fear of. It fits with the ugly clothing, the cassette carry cases full of AC/DC cassettes, the fluffy inner soles, the ski mittens – this is the truth of it: most things in op shops are hideous. Objects to make life easier that complicate it further, the specialised kitchen gizmos and boat tow ropes in brown vinyl cases labelled 'Tow Rope' in silver cursive.

Occasionally a particularly neglected object attracts my pity. After a year and a half I finally bought a Dutch copy of *Girlfriend in a Coma*, or *Vriendin in Coma*, by Douglas Coupland from Hornsby Vinnies. Every time I browsed the books I noticed the striking naked-girl cover design, picked it out, realised *Oh, this again* and thought, *No, I don't need it. I can't read Dutch.* After this process was repeated about ten times it ceased to be a book and became like an abandoned pet. Even though I didn't want to buy it, it eventually won me over and now sits on my bookshelf looking far away from home.

It is in the more cluttered shops that these objects tend to linger, among the bric a brac and the furniture. As well as *Vriendin in Coma*, Hornsby Vinnies had a print of a sad-faced boy that I deliberated over for months. I came close to buying it many times before putting it back, thinking, *No, it is too ugly*. I am often with my mother when visiting this shop, and we'd have debates about him in the car on the way home:

'I can't believe I left the boy behind again.'

'He's a horrible little boy. A little brat.'

'He's sensitive. He's filled with the pain of the world.'

'He's spoilt! He's crying because he hasn't got what he wants.'

'I should have bought him.'

Generally, when an object takes on these proportions in my mind, even if I claim to hate it, I am shattered when I return to the shop to find it gone.

After waking up with the boy on my mind yet again, I realised it was time. I decided to go and claim him. This involved a tedious train ride with long waits for connecting services, but I was resigned to it as part of my pursuit of the prize. What would I do if he was not there? I am no stranger to such fruitless missions, outcomes tumbling through my head. *Still there. Not there. Not there but finding something else as good. Walking through the door just as someone else is buying it. The shop closed, burnt down, replaced by a pet grooming salon.*

I stalled outside the shop, examining its cluttered window display. My natural reaction was to bound inside and claim the boy, but I was so terrified he had been sold that I thought if I played it cool there would be more chance of him being there. If I rushed in, he would be gone. Just inside the door a woman and her teenage daughter were looking through the shoes. 'These are almost stupid enough to be trendy,' said mum, pulling out a pair of black boots. I squeezed past them on my way to the bric a brac. Here I was greeted by yet more souvenirs from Tasmania. Every op shop contains a souvenir from Tasmania, be it a toothpick holder or a tea towel or an ashtray. One could have a complete Tasmania kitchen with a modicum of effort. Or one could collect as many souvenirs as possible, move to Tasmania, set up a roadside stall and put it all back into circulation.

This abundance of abandoned souvenirs is evidence that Tasmania exists to provide people with a place to buy useless things. From the look of these objects, mainlanders regard Tasmania as a quaint place filled with apples and Tasmanian devils and not much else. Having never been there, all I can picture of it is old cars with 'Holiday Isle' numberplates, cruising along roads lined with apple trees and waving, bearded farmers in overalls.

Why was I in a reverie about Tasmania? The boy!

I went through to the furniture section and flipped through the framed pictures. Ugly landscapes, Monet prints… not there. My spirits sank. I felt blind hatred for whoever had bought him, picturing a succession of likely culprits lovingly polishing his frame. I cast my eyes around the graveyard of wardrobes, couches, LPs and electrical gadgets in the room, feeling angry.

I looked higher. Above a rack of raincoats his tearful eyes surveyed the junk-filled room, like he was distressed by being cast into this conglomeration of old luggage and armchairs and wished someone could rescue him. That someone is me.

Place

once more, reality

kills fantasy

Turramurra Summer

The post office in the morning is like a sixty-year school reunion.

Some are hard of hearing. Some move very … very … slowly. Some move surprisingly fast and I think, 'you're too old to move that fast'.

'How are you today?'

'Awww – not bad for an old bloke.' This is one of the jolly ones. I've learnt they come in two varieties. Cheerful and Cheerless. There is no middle ground.

I like the old ladies who sit in Pierre's Patisserie, sipping cappuccinos and picking at éclairs. Their faces are garish from the wrong shade of face powder and lipstick bleeding into the wrinkles around their mouths. They wear brooches and sensible beige shoes and sit as straight as they did in classrooms in 1935, as if still fearing the cane.

I feel like I have similarities with these old folk. I'm often heard to complain 'I feel eighty years old' in crises of physical duress. I enjoy cups of tea and early bedtimes. I am grouchy when the weight of life upon me feels too much. I wear petticoats and gloves and don't swear. I believe there may well be more similarities between me and these old women than me and women my age.

Slowly my compatriots are disappearing. The two stalwarts of the Turramurra shops, The Village Gentry and Sheila Boutique, have closed down because their clientele are passing on to the next life. Sheila was the only place besides op shops that I ever saw old lady dresses for sale. Those sensible, button-through, belted floral flocks and matching cardigans. I used to imagine their names in the credits for an imaginary TV show for the North Shore elderly. *Edna dressed by Sheila Boutique. Kevin by the Village Gentry.*

Besides old people, there are a lot of teenagers. Private schoolkids for the most part, luxuriating in long summer holidays. They group together at train stations for meetings of the *I own the earth* club. The silliest conversations become supernovas. They might as well be speaking with megaphones.

My particular favourites are the young male supermarket staff at Franklins. Removed from their peer group, put in a uniform behind a cash register and forced to be polite, they become very alluring. I have fantasies about seducing them in the loading dock during their Coca Cola breaks. When I buy my groceries I blush as if my thoughts are broadcast on my forehead.

I wonder if they notice me at all? I'm at an age where teenagers don't see me unless I'm wearing something particularly outlandish. I'm out of range. In my more miserable moments I wonder why I need to think teenage boys might be interested in me. Am I going to become one of those old ladies with a twenty-year old boyfriend, the butt of everyone's jokes?

I calm myself with the reality of the situation. We'd be embarrassed. My body's far less preferable than girls of their age. Teenage boys often have dubious personal hygiene. It would be over very quickly. I'd probably have to switch from Franklins to Coles, and thus pay more for my groceries. Once more, reality kills fantasy.

✤

Let us pray.

Oh Chris, Hugh, Adam, darlings of the registers. I like to picture your bedrooms, flip through your CD collections and maths exercise books. I like it how your lives are still in suspension, how your naiveté and unwise choices are attributed to youth. I want to absorb your carefree uncertainty like I want to absorb the self assurance of the generation above me.

Praise be to Turramurra.

Where every living room has a piano, every dinner a dessert, every yard a Golden Retriever.

Where every child is orthodontically corrected.

Where the national parks hide groups of over 60s ramblers and birdwatchers inching along paths in sturdy shoes, stomachs lined with sensible breakfasts.

Where under every kitchen sink is an arsenal of cleaning products to fix any possible mishap.

Where I'm an unseasonable flower, a giant red dahlia disturbing the winter.

It feels like a great joke to stroll around the most familiar place I know. At night, packs of boys in polo shirts flirt with the neon brilliance of Quix. They're harmless, they belong in cartoons, they slam their shoulders together and hoot and honk. By midnight my street is deserted and all the houses have their lights out. My mother has instructed me to *on no account* walk home by myself after dark.

Her refrain: Anything Could Happen.

She's right, but it's nothing to be afraid of. I'd rather embrace the anything. In her estimation, because I don't have a car and a mobile phone I am unsafe after dark. In my estimation, if anyone tries to attack me, bursts out from behind a hedge or suchlike, I will gouge them with my white lace parasol right where it hurts.

I get home safely. The house has trapped the sunny day, the air is thick and hot. I don't turn on the lights because I know the house so well I can do everything in the dark. I open the windows, put on the Arcade Fire and dance in the hallway, leaning up against walls and executing moves that I'm sure look just fantastic. I might as well be in a music video. I flop onto the olive green couch, with toast and the remote control.

Rage. The new Nick Cave video with animated rabbits flopping around.

'You've gone too far,' I say out loud. My lap is full of crumbs. I'm the arbiter of taste, I can tell Old Nickers where he's going wrong.

'Nickers old chap, leave the bunny rabbits out of it.'

The video ends and I give up on television.

It's great to be by myself. I'm a love letter in an envelope, sealed up, secret. I'm a diamond ring in the belly of a fish.

Alone I've been granted deliverance from the unspeakably vulgar modern world. Any year above 2000 sounds like the setting for a speculative fiction, I try not to think of them if I don't have to. If I restrict myself to 2CH Easy 1170, wear crimplene and read 70s *Women's Weekly*s I can almost fool myself. I might learn shorthand to delude myself further.

My grandparents had this house built in 1959. In some obscure shoebox there are little green-tinged photographs of the vacant lot. They're shocking because I don't exist then, because I can't even imagine the details that could have conspired to prevent my existence. I only know major ones: my grandparents could have chosen Canada rather than Australia as their post-war British colony of choice. As a kid I thought how cool it would be to have a Canadian accent, until I realised I wouldn't exist.

I lived in this house for the last years of primary school. In my mauve-themed bedroom I liked to lie in bed making up stories about how I was an orphan who lived in an attic, based on the Frances Hodgkins Burnett story *The Little Princess*. Then, as now, I spent a lot of time lying in bed. Under it I kept cardboard boxes containing trinkets: ornaments, notebooks, papers and my beloved collection of paint sample cards arranged in colour order. The bed was positioned a few inches from the wall and I liked to lie at the edge of it and poke my arm down the gap to examine the contents of my boxes. My mother told me this covert hoarding was a sign of mental instability. The other odd thing she didn't approve of was my moss garden. I dug up sections of moss from the garden, planted them in plastic Petri dishes and lined them up on the windowsill. When the moss began to grow up the wall my garden was dismantled. She said it was bad to sleep in a room with mould spores because they'd get into my lungs. I pictured my lungs as a mossy, rainforest environment and preferred this to her description – pink flesh bags that slowly turn grey as you age, or quickly turn black if you smoke. I *still* think of this description with horror.

On the other side of the wall was my grandparents' bedroom. They had twin beds divided by a bedside table and I liked to picture their heads on the other side of the wall. My grandfather would knock on the wall before he went to sleep, 'rat tat tat tat tat' and I'd reply, 'tat tat'. Strange to think fifteen years later the same wall separates the aching shouldered, complex adult sulking at her desk from her mysterious, frantic uncle. As I try and write about Chihuahuas and he tries to scrape flaking paint.

✤

Actual conversation from the aisles of Turramurra Coles, 8.30 pm, Sunday night.

Vanessa, *surveying the large gaps in the produce department*: We've come at a bad time.

Mother *looks up from serious investigation of the avocados.*

Vanessa *points at the space where the capsicums used to be.*

Mother: Oh these people can eat around here.

Vanessa: The only potatoes left are green ones. Poison.

Mother: That's because they have them under these fluorescent lights.

Vanessa: There's beans at least.

Mother *scuttles over:* Give me a look at them. Withered little – oh, I suppose they're alright.

She continues examining the produce department, while **Vanessa** *searches for tinned vegetables. She chooses the canned tomatoes with the prettiest label.*

Mother *catches up*: Do you need anything else?

Vanessa: Oh yes, toilet paper.

Mother: Been through all that already?

Vanessa, *blushing*: Mother it's been two months! Nine rolls in two months is hardly excessive. In fact I'd say it was modest.

Vanessa selects her usual toilet paper, the environmentally responsible recycled stuff.

Mother: Oh Vanessa, get the good stuff.

Vanessa: This is the one I always get, the environmentally responsible one.

Mother: It's horrible.

Vanessa: God, I don't need toilet paper with a 250 thread count!

Mother: Well, I just like quality … How much is that stuff? *Points derisively at my toilet paper in the trolley.*

Vanessa: Three dollars twenty five.

Mother *goes to look at her preferred brand, Quilton Four-ply, and proceeds to work out the cost per roll.* **Vanessa** *doesn't want any part of this and goes in search of vanilla flavoured tea, and when she returns,* **Mother** *is peering into the freezer in search of frozen fish meals.*

Vanessa, *holding the freezer door open*: Hey remember those awful fish pies I used to like when I was a teenager? Those gooey ones with the white sauce.

Mother: Close the door, it's freezing (mutter mutter). Ice cream (mutter mutter). These people are desperate, I've never seen people shop like they do here.

Vanessa: Storming the aisles on a Sunday afternoon.

Mother: Are you sure you want to buy that horrible stuff?

Vanessa: It's made from recycled Christmas cards and office memos. I like the idea my toilet paper used to be Christmas cards.

Mother, *pretending to be shocked*: Oh Vanessa!

They approach the checkouts and are about to put their items onto the conveyor when…

Vanessa: Look! That young man's unpacking potatoes!

Mother: Let's get him.

✤

3.16 am. I awake from a humid dream and my eyes dart straight to the clock radio. The sound of the screen door swinging open and the key in the door has poked through the fabric of my dream. *Who is it?*

I lie completely motionless, as if I've been set in an iceblock. I know being still won't save me, so I think about what weapons I have within close reach. I'll have to spray French perfume in the eyes of the intruder. Whatever animal scent glands it is made of will surely sting to buggery.

No sounds follow and I become braver. I get up and turn on a light. The hallway is illuminated. Beige carpet, the camphor box, the telephone, some stranded light fittings. All completely regular. The door, of course, is shut.

More noises start up from the shed roof. It's a possum. Possums sound uncannily human as they scoot around, but now I recognise the sound I'm not afraid.

Back in bed I can't sleep. When the possum stops crashing around it's too quiet. I imagine how many other people in my street are awake at this time and why: heartbreak, illness, babies.

I spent long nights awake here as a child, because the sound of Mrs Matthews' dripping drains prevented my sleep. The regular drip-drip-drip terrified me because I thought it was the sound of footsteps. Although it was every night and I knew it was the drain, the noise scared me so much that it was impossible to get to sleep. Just the idea of hearing footsteps was enough. I longed for nights of rain when the drip was consumed by sound because these were the only nights I could sleep properly. I sometimes wonder if these years of insufficient sleep as a child sabotaged my development.

Lie in bed and try to sleep.

Lie in bed and try to sleep.

It takes hours.

Hours.

I get up early, feeling delicate as a freshly peeled boiled egg. It's a bad time to be tired because it is the day I have to get the house in order. It has to look generic for the real estate agent's appraisal and then the streams of mortgages on legs that will tramp through the rooms and fantasise about their new life. No postcard of Edvard Munch and the girlfriend who shot him through the hand stuck to the mirror. No painting of the hare that I like to joke is my moral guardian. No giant red fans or tall green glass vases.

1. People might steal things
2. The house has to be neat.
3. Neat, just plain and simple.
4. I mean I *like* your things.
5. But.

This is the day my uncle's been working towards. Every evening he's been around, fixing things. His obsession is 'doing things properly', which means concentrating on tiny details like painting the wooden edging around the kitchen benches. He tells me about this in a voice of great animation, as if he is explaining the plot of a particularly fantastic story.

Things get bad straight away when I stub my toe on the back door, which has an unusual opening mechanism to accommodate for my grandparents' lack of mobility in the last years of their life. I miss my grandparents. My toe feels broken. The box is heavy. Ugh.

Whatsthefuckenpointofanything—

I'm sobbing as I carry boxes to the shed and build them into an unstable tower. The boxes used to hold olive oil, turpentine, wine, drills, eggs, equipment for medical laboratories and televisions. Now they contain the material evidence of my existence. As countless people have reminded me, I own a lot of material evidence.

Metal Guy: So, where are you from?

Vanessa: Turramurra.

Metal Guy: Ooh, posh. What's the house like?

Vanessa: It's a twenty-bedroom mansion.

Metal Guy: Shit! You got servants?

Vanessa: Sure. I make love with the butler in the servants' quarters whilst my parents are getting private tennis lessons.

Metal Guy: haw haw haw.

Vanessa: I'm getting a unicorn for Christmas – my father is a pioneering genetic engineer and his speciality is creating mythical creatures from already existing animals.

Metal Guy: Wow, you rich chicks.

Vanessa: I've never reused a teabag or had to buy No Frills brand tampons and I think public transport is a breeding ground for germs.

Somewhere in that back garden, there's a gun.

The garden is thirty metres long and twenty wide. From it has come beans, peas, oranges, carrots, potatoes, strawberries, boysenberries, peas, mandarines and plums, but now the garden beds are reduced and straggly. The plum tree still tries, in November it was covered in small green fruit like Christmas baubles. Earlier in the year there were mandarines but the few remaining on the trees when I moved in were tough and corky, only good for throwing over the back fence and trying to hit the trunks of the gum trees in the park.

The gun was my grandfather's. In Armidale he used to shoot possums as they ambled along tree branches. I can't fit this image with my memories of him quietly tinkering with watches or sketching odd inventions while listening to *The Goon Show*, but I don't imagine he would have had trouble shooting a possum. He was always very matter of fact.

When he told me he'd buried the gun in the garden I pictured it under the lawn, wrapped in oilcloth. Worms and grubs winding their way around it and the years since it was gripped by a hand stretching into decades. I envisaged a pistol, but when I asked Mother about what kind of gun they'd had in Armidale, she told me it was a rifle. A rifle!

No one would fuck with me then.

The snobby women walking obese Labradors at 6.30 am wouldn't glare at me as I walk down the hill, makeup smudged, still half asleep from the forty-minute dozing session I've enjoyed on the first train back to the northern suburbs.

Princesses with spray tans and tiny skirts wouldn't giggle at my 70s housedresses.

I wouldn't be left on hold for ten minutes, listening to that same looped Chopin prelude that sounds like someone is knitting a scarf five centimetres in front of my eyes.

Shop assistants would stop calling me 'dear' as if they were sorry for me.

Men in nightclubs would stop putting their hands on my forearms.

Katie with a special offer from The Holiday Club would hang up quick when she heard me cock my rifle.

People will be surprised when I start to take my rifle around with me. I'll patchwork a bag for it from the little dresses I used to wear in the anorexic late 90s. If someone displeases me, I'll undo the stud at the top of the bag and poke the metal snout out the end. They won't expect such a polite, ladylike girl, who is continually asked, 'Are you English?' because she affects a posh lilt to her sentences, to be carrying a rifle. My successful passage through life will be assured.

✤

I'm making the men nervous by poking around the tables of electricals. They cast sideways looks as I examine an answering machine, large and heavy as an atlas, and tuck it under my arm.

I've never seen so much action in Turramurra. The hall is full of people sorting through junk on trestle tables, and the sound of colliding crockery and constant 'excuse me's. Above it all floats the amplified voice of Stan, who roves through the flea market with a cordless microphone, describing the fantastic value of the objects on sale in his signature doddery style.

'We've got VCRs, DVDs, CDs, VDs, VC … DC … DVDs! What's this one? Shanania Twain. We've got Shanania Twain DVDs.'

Teenage girls giggle at his mistakes, as they giggle at the sign for the sausage sizzle that reads 'meet sosajes'. I think the misspelling is a joke until I hear one of the doughy boys working the grill ask, 'Well how do *you* spell it?' What are they teaching them in those plush private schools?

I buy until I can carry no more. I keep dropping things and bumping into people, delirious from being around so many Turramurrarians and so much of their discarded stuff.

'What do we have here? 50 cents for a roll of clean, new bandage.'

Tell me about it Stan. Every one of us will need a bandage sometime in our lives. That's one hot item you've got there.

The Velodrome and the Olympia

Ducking through a hole in the saggy wire fence to get inside the grounds of the velodrome I felt I was entering somewhere I belonged. My childhood feeling of secret significance was reactivated, when simple places had the potential to be magical and my own mythology took over from the real world. The velodrome could be anything I wanted it to be. I imagined putting images of it on postcards and sending them to strangers and I dreamed of the picnics and parties and weddings I could one day have there. Lying in bed at night over the other side of Parramatta Road I liked to think of the velodrome empty, waiting for my next visit.

It didn't seem part of the factories and terrace houses in the surrounding streets. It had the same still presence as abandoned drive-in cinemas and empty sports fields, a kind of force field that turned all sound into a background blur and left me with my thoughts. Devoid of the cyclists for which it was intended the concrete track reminded me of an amphitheatre, something grand and Roman. It had the atmosphere of a ruin despite the fact it had only been there thirty years. Looking closer, the faded ads for Winfield reds along the side gave me visions of the spectators at a 1970s bicycle race. Men wearing tight t-shirts branded with beer logos or the names of tourist towns, stringy women with tanned children and full eskies. Transistor radios and sunburn.

Back then the grass would have been clipped and the advertisements neatly painted. Later, after years of disuse it appeared to be slowly melting into the ground, in chips and cracks and flakes. As the wooden stands rotted and the concrete gave over to the weeds growing through the cracks, decay seemed to be a gentle, softening force, gradually making the structures organic.

I liked to sit on the stands and look west, towards Annandale. I saw familiar landmarks from a new, elevated perspective – the spire of the Anglican church, the gaudy main road billboards and the rise and fall of the different roofs – and thought of this as the canopy that held my life in place. Or I lazily watched people walking their dogs around the perimeter of the track, fixing my eyes on Labradors and Pugs while my thoughts skipped off, untraceable. At dusk the lights of the planes coming in to land spotted the sky, gradually enlarging until they roared overhead and I waited until only the tiniest tint of daylight remained before going home.

Then a sign went up. Much as I love signs, this one accompanied a severe layer of wire fencing and featured molecules with long, carcinogenic names and the shocking news that O'Dea Reserve was contaminated. The soil presented 'a significant risk of harm to human health'. The velodrome was doomed and I felt angry, as if something had been stolen from me. It hurt to be reminded that the velodrome was not really mine. It was O'Dea Reserve, property of the council, polluted from past uses as a rubbish tip and a factory.

I wasn't scared by Polycyclic Aromatic Hydrocarbons and neither were other people because holes soon appeared in the fence. It wasn't as if we were going to eat the soil, so even if the velodrome's days were numbered it seemed unfair that people could no longer use it while it was there exactly as it had been the day before the fences and signs went up.

My first mission into the velodrome after its condemnation was also the first time I went there at night. The grass had grown to knee-height and was slowly consuming the park benches. Weeds shed sticky burrs the shape of exclamation points which covered my socks in prickles and made it difficult to walk through the long grass. The grass and the weeds were so healthy that I figured it must be the Aromatic Hydrocarbons. The contamination gave the velodrome a Chernobyl-like grandeur and the same sense of hidden danger; while everything looked regular, on a molecular level I imagined it to be the equivalent of a piranha-infested lake.

We negotiated the long grass until we came to the concrete ellipse of the velodrome. We looked like wind-up toys, all lost on our own path. Phil was carrying a brown leather briefcase full of Learn Chinese tapes that we found in a pile of rubbish during the walk from Newtown. It gave him a crazed appearance, like he was a lost businessman doomed to endlessly traverse wastelands in search of the office. I giggled as I watched him struggle through the grass in long, laboured strides, briefcase slapping at his legs. I came to a stop at one of the stands and climbed to my usual position at the top as Tim's grey shadow ran a lap around the track.

The buzz of a helicopter accompanied the circle of light that I watched moving over the factory roofs. I was sure the helicopter was searching for escaped felons, and felt frightened we would be targeted and spot-lit. They were probably looking for three people who had just robbed a bank and here we were with a big leather briefcase, tottering crazily around an abandoned site. I pictured it all in my mind: the wind from the chopper blades and the megaphones and the questioning. But the searchlight came to the edge of the velodrome and no further. The helicopter changed direction. We were safe.

I moved from the stands down into the flat grassy oval at the centre of the track. I felt tiny down here, as small as an olive in the middle of a large serving plate. Phil joined me and we stood in wordless appreciation of night and space, heads tilted towards the few stars strong enough to shine through the ambience of the city.

'Hey!' Tim's voice ballooned over to us. He was at the top of the steepest edge of the track. 'Come up here!'

'I can't climb that,' I whined, but he persisted and stretched his hand down for me to grasp. When I tried to climb I was surprised that it wasn't very difficult. I have little faith in my physical abilities, to the point where I rarely test them, so I was proud of myself as I stood on the top, surveying the velodrome. The lights that circled the track were all broken, the wires hanging down, creaking in the breeze. Behind that was the sound of the traffic, the ever-present roar of the city. We stood there for a long time, just looking. It felt good to be in this unusual place, with no one else in sight, after midnight, the whole suburb sleeping.

A few months later Tim arrived at my house with the news.

'Velodrome's gone.'

I felt sick and resigned and avoided walking past it for weeks, until curiousity overtook melancholy. Everything had been uprooted, a grubby yellow earthmover slowly shunted pieces of what had been the concrete track into piles. I remembered a time I lay on it half asleep, enjoying the sun, and thought how that piece would be somewhere in the rubble.

The ground was being levelled, so there would be no hint of its former shape. People would move into the area for the first time without knowing that, a few years earlier, they would have lived near this surprising place. For them it is now a playground carpeted in soft, foamy asphalt to stop kids from getting hurt when they fall off the ultra-safe equipment. Even if they were told what it used to be, it probably wouldn't mean much. Hearing descriptions of what places used to be like has an airiness, for it is impossible to imagine them properly and you inevitably disappoint the person who reverently describes it. I am aware that it probably doesn't sound like an extraordinary place every time I tell someone about it, but often significant places are not extraordinary. Whatever image of the velodrome you might have in your mind, what is more important is that you understand the sense that it gave me, that it was special and different, somewhere I could go to feel removed from my everyday life yet also feel at home.

Existing now only in my memory and a few photographs (I look so young with my red streaked hair and inches of black plastic bangles) I find I can still retreat there, as I try to remember exactly how it felt to lean down and duck under the fence and walk inside. Like I try to recall the details of the houses I grew up in, many of them now also demolished, by thinking of how the atmosphere changed when I walked through the door, from outside to in.

Significant places have always grabbed me like this. Once I cross their boundaries I feel a shift as the relationship between myself and my surroundings is amplified. I'm in it and it's in me.

With the velodrome gone I looked to the other places that give me a similarly charged feeling. They are usually decaying in one way or another: junkyards, parks built over old rubbish tips and old shops that creakingly continue to function, like the Olympia Milk Bar on Parramatta Road in Stanmore.

I look for the Olympia every time I pass by. To not look would be akin to ignoring a special password. Like a ghost, to take my eyes off it would make it disappear, dissolve into vapour. Peering in past the grimy windows, mended with pieces of wood nailed over each other, past the piles of dusty chocolate boxes and into the gloom, I look for the man at the heart of this decrepit palace.

He spends all day behind the counter, an apron over his neat but worn clothes, waiting for the few customers that come in for a two-dollar milkshake or cup of tea or a can of Coke (he does not stock Diet Coke). Behind him is a wall of shelves packed with chocolate boxes, the display kind that holds individual bars for sale. Once I made the error of pointing to a Cherry Ripe box and asking to buy one, only for him to tell me in taciturn, almost monosyllabic tones that in fact he had only three chocolate bars in stock, white chocolate Kit Kats, Rolos, or plain Cadbury Dairy Milk. It was then I realised that practically all the chocolate boxes were empty.

I pass the Olympia in the bus almost every day, and almost every time someone sitting nearby starts to talk about it. As it becomes more and more dilapidated and more and more anachronistic, with its 50s-style furnishings and fading 80s ads for Pepsi clear cola on the walls, people's interest in it has grown.

'Look at that!' from those who've never seen it before.

'That guy. He's been there forever. Must make no money at all,' from locals making conversation.

'Milk bar's still there,' from the infrequent Parramatta Road traveller.

'Looks like a horror movie in there,' from a schoolgirl, giggling to her new boyfriend.

Some people have nicknames for him. 'Oh, you mean Drac?' says a friend when I explain my interest in the milk bar, a reference to the proprietor's vampiric appearance. Opinions vary as to whether he's a nice old man or a tyrannical grouch.

Many are too scared to enter. Others, like me, are addicted to looking up every time I go by and wondering through what kind of magic this place still exists.

The first time I noticed the Olympia I was instantly obsessed. This was when I was still unfamiliar with the area and out on a scouting mission. From a distance I saw the old sign hanging from the awning: MILK SNACK BAR, SMOKES SWEETS. I expected it to be one of the usual slightly dingy but still functioning Parramatta Road stores that had seen better days. It was this taken to the extreme. Looking beyond the landslide of empty chocolate boxes in the window display I found my face uncomfortably close to that of an ageing man with greyish skin and sprouting black eyebrows. He had a severe expression and I looked away, unnerved. He didn't look as if my scrutiny of his chocolate boxes pleased him one bit. I looked at the fold out painted sign in the doorway, 'Come on in for Tea!' Despite being a bit scared, I decided to do just that.

The interior felt oppressive, despite the high ceilings. The one functioning fluorescent tube on the ceiling provided little light and the patina of age over everything made me feel too bright and clean and modern, like I was disturbing a museum display rather than preparing myself to enjoy the pleasure of a cup of tea. Walking into the Olympia I had the distinct feeling that I was stepping into this man's head, the dusty corners and empty boxes were hidden memories and to look out at the street was to look through his eyes. As soon as I entered he stood alert at the counter, acknowledging me with a nod, awaiting my order. I was to find out the hard way that he doesn't like his store to be scrutinised, doesn't allow photographs, and doesn't answer questions about the history of his shop.

I like this about it, that it is a mystery and may always remain so. After being reprimanded for taking a photo and apologising many more times than was necessary, I respected his desire to go unrecorded. I like the fact that no well-meaning local historian has bustled in with a microcassette recorder and a digital camera and convinced him to relate His Story, which would most likely be packaged as *so much has changed, the old ways were simpler.* Just because he's old and his milk bar has been the same for the last forty years doesn't mean he has an obligation to talk about it. Over the course of many visits I have realised that as far as he's concerned he's just running his shop, living his life the way he has for decades.

Of course, not having the truth to intervene enables me to gather evidence and make up stories to my heart's desire. My personal dossier of Olympia mythology is vast. The subject of how he came to spend all of his time alone in his shop is a big source of speculation. Upon noticing the old sign for the 'Nutri Tonic Perms' offered by the Olympia Salon upstairs, I decided that his wife used to work as a hairdresser. It was after her death that he became so aloof and began to collect empty boxes. Looking at the first floor windows from across the street I imagine the shadowy abandoned hairdressing equipment inside, shrouded in spider webs. On sunny afternoons, though, the light slants into them in such a way for me to see that they are empty, like the chocolate boxes.

Whatever the truth is, it will be disappointing. For all my excitement the day I encountered him in the newsagency across the road, the first and only time I have ever seen him outside the milk bar, it made me realise that he is just a person. He sleeps, dreams, eats, remembers, reads ... he bought the Daily Telegraph from the newsagency, then jaywalked across the busy morning peak hour six-lane Parramatta Road! I was horrified and fixed my eyes on him to will him safely across.

The sadness of the Olympia Milk Bar is that with his death it will be no longer. There will be a write-up in the *Sydney Morning Herald*, the fixtures will be sold off to retro dealers and the building will become a Vespa showroom. I feel that this will mark the day I leave Sydney to its shiny metropolis future and move somewhere else. I find it beautiful and heartbreaking that he doesn't disappear, that he remains as an anachronism, although it is painful to look for him every day, knowing that the day will come when I look and he will not be there. He seems so fragile in there with the world thundering around him, the relentless traffic roaring past. One time, asking for a bottle of water, my voice was drowned by a semi-trailer screaming past and he shook his head to indicate he hadn't heard.

'So much traffic!' I said.

'Too much,' he replied quietly.

I wonder what will be unlocked when the Olympia is gone. Everyone who knows the area has an Olympia story, it is a conversation topic that cannot fail. Standing in backyards at parties, searching for something to say to a beautiful stranger in front of me, I can do a lot worse than 'you know that milk bar ...'. To those that haven't ever been in there, I meticulously recount the experience.

Sitting at one of the tables and sipping tea in the gloom I feel nervous, suspecting that he doesn't really want me in there. I watch him out of the corner of my eye, standing at the counter or sweeping open the door to the cavernous back room, as if to check on something out there. I imagine this back room could have been a dance hall in more cheerful days. Occasionally

I've come in when he's been listening to Greek radio or grilling chops in the kitchen out the back and these details delight me because they make him seem less alone. Usually, however, he is waiting behind the counter. What must he think about all day, standing there, watching the traffic pass on Parramatta Road? People walk in and immediately exclaim, 'Oh my GOD!' Schoolkids giggle and people stand and stare. It is as if he is on display. I am no better than any of these people, as I sit admiring the pale blue laminex tables with matching chairs, the long curved counter, the faded signs politely suggesting milkshake flavours and the now defunct neon sign at the back of the store that outlines, 'Late Suppers, Steak Sandwiches'.

The days when the Olympia offered steak sandwiches are long in the past. These days it is either a milkshake in a dented metal cup or a cup of tea in a grimy pink teacup. Rumours of someone eating a tomato and cheese sandwich in there recently I dismissed as a fabrication, created purely to taunt me.

I collect all the slivers of Olympia experiences and information, all the things people say about it as we pass it in the bus, all the times I've been in there and the different people I've taken there, my sightings of him doing things other than standing behind the counter (exciting things such as cleaning the windows and mopping the floor). I wonder what I'm building by collecting all this. Although I feel cynical about the local historian with microcassette recorder figure, I feel that the Olympia is important enough for me to want to save it through my memories. Despite this, I write with trepidation, knowing that he would probably hate the idea of me musing on my observations of him for other people to read.

For he is already living his life in public, always visible as people walk past and gawk at him like he's an exhibit in a wax museum. Some of these people are offended and cry out, 'He doesn't sell anything', as if by the virtue of being a shop it should be neat, clean and ready to accommodate the customer. These people miss the point. It is not really a shop at all. The milk bar is the man, waiting out the rest of his life behind a counter, alone with his thoughts, whatever they might be.

Postcards and the Colour Wheel

I'm wearing an electric blue tracksuit, pedalling on an exercise bike and reading a ragged ex-library travel guide for Portugal. I'm under the house surrounded by the disassembled, the unplugged, the boxed. The air smells of dust and damp.

– The hidden life of suburbia.

Do other people expend such effort describing to themselves what they are doing as they are doing it? I like to caption myself as if I'm an illustration in a children's encyclopaedia. To get to this image there would be a drawing of me dragging the bicycle home from a pile of junk outside a four-bedroom brick veneer. Then a thought bubble filled with kitsch dreams: sweatbands and a bottle of one calorie TAB for when I've cycled ten virtual kilometres. At the end of the sequence is me with my new muscular body lifting a Volkswagen above my head using only one hand.

– I'm just down in the basement, honey. I'm reading up on our vacation.

The imaginary midday movie in my head.

– *Portugal Dos Pes…quin…tos?* This miniature village sounds just neat-o!

The miniature village is weird. A tribute to colonial conquests, the first section is decorated by six-foot tall fibreglass eggs. Red and blue eggs decorate the top of the miniature cathedral, a yellow egg is mounted on a plinth in the courtyard of a Moorish palace, yet another is positioned among a nest of sticks in the middle of a path. One is propped up beside a Coke machine as if dumped there and forgotten. Some brooms are stacked against it. I put my ear to the shell, hoping to hear the stirring of a baby orc inside, ready to peck its way out and make off with some of the Pesquintos.

The Pop Singer and I pause in front of a giant fibreglass map where continents swim in a sea the colour of backyard swimming pools. Australia is hidden behind a bronze statue of an imperious explorer, ignored by the coloured lines that mark conquest and trade between continents. It sits there like an extra puzzle piece.

– Poor Australia.

– It's like something fallen down the back of the couch.

In the next section of the village the eggs are still mounted in odd places but now there is one crucial difference: they have cracked in half. Instead of palaces there are many tiny cottages that I crawl into to the bemusement of children, who wait for me to squeeze out of the little doorways with looks of utter confusion. I dictate the photographs that are to be taken of me, hoping they will capture my delighted confusion. I like the idea of myself as a giant, so I make good use of the miniature village and the globe of the world with questionable placement of New Zealand.

– Stand there and take a photo of me pointing at it. Wait for these people to go past … Now.

I try to smile but can only look confused. Palaces turn to cottages, the world goes from flat to round, the eggs are broken? I try to relax into the surreality of it.

What a relief – I do not have to decode everything. I can doze off to the coo and hiss of another language with no demands made upon my comprehension. Like a child I can choose between striving to understand or retreating to my imagination where I reconstruct what I perceive according to my own rules. Home is a daydream.

In Coimbra, when I try to buy a stamp for my postcard, the lady at the newsstand is unconvinced by 'Australia' and insists that I need a stamp for Austria. As her scowl deepens the man behind me comes to the rescue and assures her that this 'Australia' exists and I need a Rest-of-the-world stamp, rather than a Europe one. To punish me she gives me as many stamps as possible to stick on the card, so I have only a tiny space to write my message. She does not like the sound of 'Australia'.

Hi Friend, I'm in a place where Australia doesn't exist! This postcard will be floating around Austria before the dead letter office puts it out of its misery, love VB.

On my friends' fridges, held in place by magnets for local plumbing services, I am reunited with my postcards. I turn them over in my hands, note their postmarks and worn edges. The messages seem remote, although only written a few weeks beforehand. Was I really in a summer night, watching a handsome boy read Derrida at a cafe in Coimbra, when a raucous group of singing scouts tramped past brandishing rakes, picks and sacks?

They gathered in rival groups, the reds against the blue and whites, and I waited for them to run against each other, tools aloft, screaming war.

My messages form a complete catalogue, dispersed among my friends. Disappointment in the Lisbon glove shop. Blood and Guts. Cherry Brandy in Medicine Cups. Portuguese Goths. For the first time I was the explorer relaying details back home. At any time at least one of my friends must be exploring so I can pin my dreams to them; for these weeks I was living my own dream. It had always seemed impossible to me that I would ever make it overseas, that, if the plane didn't plummet into the ocean on the way there, I'd drop dead as soon as I stepped foot in another country. It would be a tragic story: *First time overseas, been wanting to go all her life and then, wham, DEAD.*

I was partly disappointed at my lack of obliteration. I fulfilled the correct requirements of travel I had always been on the receiving end of: observing, sending scraps back home. Re-reading my postcards I imagine the images that must have formed in people's minds when they received them. The 'I'm very happy' I write on a postcard to my mother becomes a sore point when I break up with the Pop Singer. She thinks I've made the wrong decision and shakes this sentence like a rattle, as if he had single-handedly built Europe for my delectation.

I was happy because I was living entirely in the present, because people were passionately haggling over fox skins at the flea market, because the details from my Year 7 French textbook came alive in bottles of Orangina, because I was drunk on cherry brandy and the cobblestones were warm on my back when I lay down in the main square to look at the rearranged stars above. More than any person or place I was in love with being alive. With my heartbeat, my vision, my thoughts, the electricity snaking along my nerves.

✣

There are stores that sell only birdcages or men's hats or ribbons. The tram squeezes in between them, threatening to graze the corners of the buildings. I imagine I am inside a toy and being directed by a giant hand as it skates down inclines and clunks around corners.

Of all the stores it is the glove shop I like the best. It is the size of a walk-in wardrobe and sells only one style of glove in different colours.

– Red please.

– You are like all the women. All the women want red.

He goes into a back room and after a minute I lean forward over the counter to check what he is doing. He is in front of a wall of drawers marked by paper labels held with metal clips, intent on the luminous keypad of his mobile phone. He's sending a text message! I'm upset he is perverting my fantasy of being a stylish 40s lady with his modern gizmo. Message sent, he chooses a box of red and burgundy gloves and brings it to the counter. Flipping through them he reports that they only have small sizes left. I stick out my hand to try one nevertheless.

– I prepare first.

He inserts a wooden implement that looks like a large, blunt pair of scissors into the glove to stretch it open, finger by finger. He positions my elbow on a small round cushion, raises my hand and squeezes the glove onto it. He tries to smooth the leather down over each finger but there is no way it will fit me. I look at the tiny red glove half on my hand and concede defeat. He offers me a business card by way of consolation. I retreat past the window display of delicate sets of coloured hands crossed over each other, like captured gestures of ladies at the opera.

✥

Restaurants announce their tortures in glass cabinets containing gory scenes. A ribcage squirms with different tones of blood and gristle. Limp fish droop. A fowl so large I cannot guess what bird it once was slumps under a layer of bluish fat. 'Carcasses everywhere,' I say in disgust, as the combined sizzle of grills at dinnertime fills the streets and the bins fill with pig legs. The only live animals around are inedibly scrawny mongrel dogs.

Vegetarian restaurants resemble hospital canteens. Young women wearing hairnets guard lukewarm food in bain-maries and customers pick at piles of plastic trays, cutlery and napkins. The restaurants are located in obscure residential districts and require much consultation of maps to find them. The diners look pale and harried and it is not surprising, considering that once outside they are confronted with flesh cabinets, flashing neon chicken carcasses, baked pig heads in the windows of cafes.

– What are they?

– Oh God. Surely not? Wolves? Look away.

✤

I lean against the wall, casting my eyes around the dungeon before focussing on my glass of absinthe. I feel woozy after a few sips, imagining the intense green invading my blood and warping my vision so everything glows with an aura.

We watch people enter, scan the room, then disappear into corners to wait. Groups of girls dressed in fluffy petticoats sit in tight circles, leaning conspiratorially forward. They remind me of dolls in national dress released from their display boxes, limbs untied to fiddle with cigarettes and the ribbons that decorate their clothing. Waiting for new people to enter, for drugs to work, for a good song to play, for the right time to make a declaration, for *something* to happen …

A boy dressed in black shreds sways back and forth on the dancefloor, a drink dangling from his hand as if held by one thread. The cloying bass and woe-is-me synthesisers have invaded his body, he sways back and forth for hours. Every time I look in that direction his presence is as relentless as the minor chords.

We join him for 'London Calling', bouncing in between the lacy girls, miming the words with as much post-apocalyptic horror as we can muster. Then we flee into the skinny, steep Lisbon streets, where people spill from tiny bars and the air is full of chatter. The goths are still contained in their cellar, waiting for something to happen as we step into the hotel elevator and wait for it to drag us to the fourth floor. All over the city, people tucked into pockets, waiting.

✤

Outside the cherry brandy bar the ground is littered with sticky plastic medicine cups and cherry pits. A man clings onto the Pop Singer's arm and screams 'Muito, muito felicidade' and wants to embrace him. I do nothing more useful than giggle.

– Is he saying happy birthday?

– Who knows?

We shake him off, tempted across the black and white cobblestones by large neon ice creams on shop awnings and the splash of the fountain in the main square. We take photos in front of the fountain, posing as if we've come ashore from a cruise fifty years ago.

At night Lisbon feels tiny, as if I could take giant steps across it from the top of one hill to another. At sunset it folds in upon itself and every dawn unfurls like origami. The bread truck painted with Virgin Marys rattles to life in the street below our window, and looking out as the sun begins to roast the roofs, I think of everything hidden beneath them.

Our guesthouse is on the top of a hill, accessed by a steep set of winding stone stairs known as 'The Backbreaker'. I count as I climb, but after two hundred I can barely breathe. Below me roof tiles mosaic and aerials swizzle-stick in my exhausted vision.

On our first night the man in charge of the guesthouse explained the strange neighbouring houses.

– They are – how you say – fraternity?

The Real República Rás-Te-Parta has effigies dangling from the roof and household appliances strung up by power cords from the front fence. On one side of the gate hangs a toilet seat, on the other a chair. This warns us civilisation is digested within, like the skulls outside Baba Yaga's hut warn travellers they risk consumption of their souls. As we walk past, weak from our ascension of The Backbreaker, a woman on the footpath in front of The

Real Republica screams a vicious tirade. A boy with dreadlocks stands on the porch, a lean toothy dog snarling behind his legs. Her ripped skirt and oranges rolling into the gutter, his smooth chest crawling with tattoos. He looks as if he cares not a whit whether his hounds demolish passers by or not.

– What do you think he's studying?

– Piracy.

I accelerate, frightened by the pirate students, hoping to come across a distracting treasure. Portuguese towns resemble flea markets, where walking is like sorting through a pile of miscellaneous, surprising objects. I get my treasure. Through a bookstore window a man in a dark suit laughs into a large black telephone. Among the mirrors and crucifixes and ancient dusty books he is difficult to detect, so for a moment the laugh seems disembodied. Further down the street tiny old ladies scuttle into houses. Washing drips from high windows and blesses my cheek with soap-scented tears – look up! The sky so blue, the sun so relentless that no object can retain colour. It is a shock to see a bright red car drive by, for most reds are that of faded Coke cans beside highways. Colourful things have to be stored carefully, in boxes wrapped in cloth in chests of drawers, so the sun does not steal their essence.

✜

The music room has yellow velvet chairs arranged like lilypads.

'It took five days for eight men to carry the queen's piano from her other palace to this one,' Tiago, the guide, tells us. I listen attentively as he goes through the Portuguese royal family tree, pointing to the corresponding portraits on the wall behind him.

'He is not handsome,' he says, as we behold King Joao VI, a hideously ugly man with googly eyes, heavy jowls and a large gut contained in tight white breeches.

'And the painter probably improved his looks in the portrait,' I say, trying to appear clever. Tiago grins and tells me that the king only had three baths in his life: at birth, before marriage and after death. Joao VI's portrait should be printed on postcards along with this fact to inspire people who feel ugly and unlovable.

He was, however, rich. The palace has twelve-hundred rooms and appears endless. I gasp at the room in which everything is made out of antlers and hides. The sofa has boar heads for arm rests. Mentally disassembling the chandeliers, chairs, tables and candelabras, I picture a herd of deer running in the forest. The shadows of the antlers make a thicket of brambles on the ceiling and I ponder how terrifying it would be to spend a night in this room. In fact the whole palace is vast and ghostly no matter which room we enter.

'The king and queen did not lie down to sleep, because they believed it was too much like death,' Tiago says when I question the strange short beds in the royal bedchamber.

When we reach the nursery, Tiago shows us the bed of the last king of Portugal and asks, 'Do you remember his name?'

'Manual II!' I shriek in delight and Tiago looks proud. It is his first tour in English and I want to be the best tourist I can. As well as the Pop Singer and I there is a Dutch family who make jokes about us having antler furniture in our house. They love trying out the wooden resting posts for the friars, which kept them upright during day-long mass to make it appear as if they were standing the whole time.

I am sad to leave Tiago at the end of the tour. I shake his hand but I want to embrace him and kiss him on the cheeks. I imagine him driving back to Lisbon in a tiny red car with pop music on the stereo, going home to his museum guide girlfriend to tell her how successful his first tour in English was. In fact I am jealous of Tiago's girlfriend and imagine what it would be like to be in her place, putting my arms around him as he is ironing a shirt or stirring a pot of soup, buying him little presents.

Ah Tiago, you exist over the other side of the world right now, never to know the garlanded place you hold in my memory. I try to remember your face properly, but it is a blur of dark hair and sharp cheekbones. I hope you and your girlfriend graduate from travel agent school and set up a lovely travel agency together.

This is one of the wonderful things about being alive: at any time, somebody you least suspect might be thinking of you. Somebody you have never met is recalling your face, you are the star of somebody's thoughts and you will probably never know about it.

I'm so guilty of this

Lawn is a substance I have invented. People I meet in bars have great difficulty understanding what I am talking about. I dip a toothpick in absinthe and draw on napkins. They laugh at me and stop speaking English so I won't bother them with crazy talk any longer.

The cobblestones that pave the city were laid by prisoners. As I walk over them I imagine the crimes committed by the hands that placed the stones. After days of walking I can feel the hard edges through my shoes, grating against my bones. My feet throb every time I sit down, which I do at every possible opportunity. When I see the silhouette of soft, plush couches through the doors of the Gulbenkian Museum, I accelerate in anticipation.

Inside the museum I stare at a display of ancient Greek coins, glowing silver under tiny buds of light. It is quiet in this section, people rush through to the Rubens and Gainsboroughs and I joke that Ancient and European Art is a good place for trysts. It is usually deserted and kisses can remain secret.

Examining the outlines of noses and chins I feel a shiver that these were once living people existing in a present, without thinking of a world in which they would be a museum exhibit. I feel insignificant staring at them, knowing that no matter how carefully ancient civilisations are reconstructed, it is impossible to know what it was like to be the curly haired man on the coin. My face is so close to the glass that my breath clouds it, trying to force our worlds together by simple proximity. My nose bumps the glass and shocks me with cold. Our worlds are utterly separate.

I am distracted by a window looking out onto – no it can't be – it's grass! Outside I take off my shoes and relish the cool smoothness of it underfoot. I realise I was spoilt growing up in the Sydney suburbs, for I could feel the sensation of grass underfoot at any time. Here it is a rare thing that gives people smiles and makes kids tumble as parents track them with long-snouted cameras. I frolic in my new yellow sundress, tossing pieces of supermarket bread roll to the ducks in the pond and wishing I could cartwheel.

✥

Before sleep a procession of faces trails through my mind. The kings of Portugal, faces in portraits, the faces of statues, of sculptures, of people on postcards and advertisements. Then the train conductor, the waiters, the hairnet girls, the ticket sellers, the newsstand lady, the boy in the internet cafe who made the Pop Singer a toasted sandwich with a pile of potato crisps on the side, the woman behind the desk at the Pensão Londres to whom we surrendered our key every time we went out. I chose the Pensão Londres because I read that it was the preferred choice of 'actors, musicians, famous television personalities'. We hoped to see Portuguese Leonard Cohens but alas – bright eyed families eating bread rolls in the dining room at 8 am.

Six months later most are vague impressions. Although there are exceptions, as there are occasionally handsome train conductors.

What this man is doing working as a train conductor is a mystery to me. He punches my ticket, I want to ask for his autograph. I think how I will never see him again, rubbing the hole in the ticket over the pad of my thumb and watching his slim hips progress through the carriage.

I fall in love with the train conductor returning from Cascais, where I fell in love with my own image. Red and white dress, red sunhat, white sunglasses, red lollipop, sitting on top of a wall overlooking the beach. An American girl asks if she can take a photo of me.

– You look interesting.

Right at this moment, I could be part of someone's slide night in Michigan.

– She said she was English, heir to a cleaning products fortune. Interesting huh?

✜

We have travelled on a bus full of laughing, tanned teenagers, through a pine forest dappled in bushfire light, our eyes drooping from lack of oxygen, to a room with twin beds wearing pink covers. I fall onto one immediately but the Pop Singer is eager for us to get to the Atlantic.

The beach is covered with umbrellas and baking bodies. The sea stretches out a defiant blue, too cold for swimming despite it being the middle of summer. People look at the ocean from the water's edge, wincing when it touches their feet. I step in and my feet scream from a cold so intense I cannot tell if they are on fire or frozen.

I bury them in the gritty sand and watch a woman with a giant cylinder strapped to her back stepping through the groups of people, singing a chant ending in 'Ameri*can*', followed by the little boy behind her carolling 'azucar, zucar!'. She is selling waffles, he is selling lollipops, yellow and green candy atop a toothpick.

I lie on the sand and pretend I am made of stone as the Pop Singer mumbles, 'This place is so obscure I can't remember its name.' I cannot either. I move my attention to an old lady sitting on a nearby deckchair making lace, loops of white frothing from her crochet hook, as the perfect Italian couple beside her arrange themselves on a towel and bake their gleaming flat bellies.

At night we wander around the town and the large houses that line the streets remind me so much of the northern beaches of Sydney I am surprised when the woman at the bar cannot understand us and gives me a spitefully strong rum and coke. She refuses to give over the remainder of the can of coke she had poured only an inch from and sets it carefully behind the bar, out of our reach.

That's right. We are in Portugal.

We make up slogans for TV ads. The ads would look as if they were filmed in the 70s then stored in a damp cupboard for thirty years.

Portugal: Always a few more stairs than you were expecting.

Portugal: Another shop window, another carcass.

Portugal: Where everything from our coffees to our elderly citizens can fit in your pocket.

Portugal: Where the beautiful boys and girls work on public transport.

✤

Watching the blue of the harbour I sink my teeth into an egg tart. A line from a trashy magazine article about one man's miracle weight loss flashes to mind: 'Remember, the first bite tastes the same as the last.' I ponder how this is an utter fallacy as my tastebuds convulse around the sweet, warm custard and the crackly pastry. This is my reward for the institutional vegetarian restaurants, the lukewarm seitan dishes, the miserable supermarket lunches of foul pickled vegetables and sawdust bread rolls.

I lie back and watch the tiny cars cross the bridge like droplets of rain shaking across a car window. I feel calm, for once not worrying about how to put things into words, licking cinnamon off my fingers, camera forgotten, everything forgotten but the pleasure of warmth and sugar, blue sky over a blue harbour.

✤

The backpack is emptied, our travelling clothes churn inside the washing machine. I drink duty-free Absolut with tap water and ice, resenting the fact the Pop Singer is more interested in sleep. Something is wrong. The happiness

I felt returning to Sydney in the yellow sundress is dissolving no matter how hard I try to cling to it.

A month later we have ceased phone calls and exchanged leftover belongings. I get it all back, even the shower cap printed with roses. I imagine the weight these objects would have had in his hands, like they were livers, hearts, as he went around his house collecting them.

Thinking of our travels is intolerable, I score it out of my mind, and when people ask for stories I gloss over them. To linger is akin to slowly peeling off a bandaid.

– How was Portugal?

– Beautiful. The sun was very bright and the old people were very short.

I am disgusted at my flippancy, but the memory of my dissolution from the Pop Singer overrides everything else. The only time I can think about the places we've been is lying in bed before sleep. This is the only time there is enough space in my mind to face the enormity of my feelings.

I imagine certain street corners and think how at that moment people are right there, pausing, passing, seeing the scene for the first time or the thousandth time, how this place exists inside the imagination of countless people and how complex it is in mine: yellow funicular, flyers for restaurants littering the ground, fading signs, graffiti, cobblestones, steep paths, broken glass to stop the pigeons, eyes wider, the terrible and beautiful feeling of possibility, that my life had collided with his, that no one else knew where we were, that new places could continue to swallow me up like this one, that the world had become three-dimensional.

Detail

TrAiNiNg my mEmorY

so i CØuLD TurN iT on
ÅNd off åt WiLL

A Journey into Deepest, Darkest Detail

Imagine writing one day and including everything, following every thought to its end.

Initially this wasn't what I intended to do. In 1997 I was part of a project in which a group of zinewriters posted something to each other at the beginning of every month. I chose this particular something by chance. May 23rd 1997 was an inauspicious day I spent waiting at home for a lady to come and look at a pram my mother had advertised in the *Trading Post*. Thinking of what I could make for the project, I used the blank afternoon to devise a kind of extended postcard of my day. I called it *Laughter and the Sound of Teacups*, a name chosen by opening the book I was reading (Philip Larkin's *Jill*) and poking my finger onto a random line. I was nineteen years old. If anyone had called me a writer I would have scoffed.

As these beginnings suggest, *Latsot* (its pleasingly snappy abbreviated title) relied on the unconscious and the instinctual. I didn't pause to examine motives or consequences, or to question whether anyone would want to read about my life. I just assumed people would, because the everyday life of strangers was the kind of thing that I found interesting.

The mail exchange project faltered, but the zine firmly established itself as part of my life. I enjoyed the focus it gave me, the mechanical pleasure of regular photocopying and posting and the feeling of connection that came with releasing it for people to read.

At the time I was living in the upstairs half of a vast crumbling terrace house, walls stuck all over with pictures, drawings, quotes, newspaper headlines and shopping lists. I aimed to make the space around me reflect the space inside my head; both were cluttered. I was an eccentric, over thinking, early-twenties housewife, with a lot of time to dream.

Laughter and the Sound of Teacups couldn't have existed in any other way but as a zine. Zines were maps of possibilities and making them I felt bold and important. Their energy came from the fact they could be utterly silly or utterly morbid, epic or throwaway – they could be anything. They were almost always heartfelt, a reflection of their creator's desires.

I used my zine to celebrate minutiae, the kinds of things that are only remembered in the moment, before being lost underneath the surge of the present. I wanted *Latsot* to act as a net for thoughts, capturing the twists and wisps that curled through my mind on any day. When I read *The Mezzanine* by Nicholson Baker, I understood his desire to quantify thought, to record everything and it spurred me on further. I challenged myself to see how deeply I could go into detail, how accurately I could chart twenty-four hours.

After the early light-hearted sketches, issues became increasingly eidetic in their detail. After every 23rd I'd write a chain of notes, to later reconstitute into the long story of what happened to me that day. I worked hard to remember everything so I wouldn't have to interrupt the day itself with note-taking, training my memory so I could turn it off and on at will. Turning on my memory meant that I was able to remember pretty much everything that happened. I would mentally build a great, cumbersome necklace, where each unit of thought suggested the next. I could embed thoughts in my mind like poking smarties into cupcake icing.

I wanted to illuminate every moment, make drama out of the everyday. Although I kept it a secret and never wrote about it directly, my life at that time was limited by illness, intense periods of fatigue that made me feel separated from the majority of my healthy, capable peers. I didn't have experiences which I felt stood up to 'What do you do?' from relatives and old high-school rivals; things like overseas travel, a stunning university career or involvement in community organisations. But if I could write about LCD displays, taxi drivers and toast as if they were as defining, it didn't matter that they were just little things.

However at the time I made no such justifications, and describing the project as a kind of self-becoming feels reductive. I wrote every issue passionately. I was diving deeper into a love affair with details and I wanted to take other people with me. I wasn't focussed on self revelation. Although it seemed like I was giving the reader license to crawl into my skin for a day, it was more that I was a frame people could peek through than a picture to be examined.

It was impossible for me to live a 23rd as if it were just any other day. Everything was heightened, anticipating memorialisation. I could feel a nebulous net of people around me, the hundred sets of eyes that would later skim over the description of my failure to make *pan de muerto* or reminiscence of what band t-shirts I owned as a teenager. I felt almost like each 23rd was my birthday. It gave me the same feeling of secret pleasure.

Each issue was a letter, to everyone and no one in particular, written with love. Which is why, for a long time, I didn't really consider it to be 'proper' writing. For me writing was about premeditation and crafting. *Laughter and the Sound of Teacups* was more like a museum display. It came from the collector part of me, the child who hoarded unlikely things and spent car journeys counting the number and type of squashed cans she saw on the roadside.

By 2002 I'd been writing fiction for a while, considering its building blocks. The *Latsots* were still gushing forth, longer and more detailed than ever (hitting the summit of 14500 words in January), but rather than a collection of field notes, I began to consider them as pieces of writing.

I am not trying to suggest that writing involuntarily is more noble or honest or effective than writing as a considered practice, but when I found myself automatically clicking into my *Latsot* 'style' and wondering about my impact as a character, I realised it was time to stop.

I no longer wanted to say everything, indeed I felt I was drowning in detail. With every issue I wrote I knew I could have gone further, said more. While this challenge had excited me, it became increasingly remote from what I was interested in. I had crafted a particular way of seeing and awareness of thought through my project, but I felt I had come to a point where my apprenticeship was over. I had wrestled with detail and now I wanted to retreat and think about different ways I could write, using what I had learnt. So, abruptly, I sent death notices to everyone on my mailing list:

> *I feel that I have written* Laughter and the Sound of Teacups *for long enough. Sixty-seven of them exist, I look at them and feel heavy from all the details and ideas contained within. I think that if I don't end it now, they will become hackneyed, and I don't want to cling onto the concept as if writing about my life is more important than my life itself.*
>
> *It has been difficult to think of a good way to end this. I liked the idea of one final grand day, summing up all I have achieved over the last five-and-a-half years, drawing all the themes together neatly. This is how life works in fiction, but despite how much of a character I may seem in my writing, I am a real- life girl with many things I still wouldn't share with anybody. I couldn't think of a good way to sum everything up, because I would have to step*

> *outside of myself and view things as if I were a character, and all the days in between each 23rd were a shadowy waiting period before the one illuminated twenty-four hours.*

I felt an equal measure of relief and sadness once I stopped and the weird, haunted feeling of giving up something that was habitual. Even now on the 23rd of the month I feel uncomfortable flutters that there is something I should be doing, a nervous rush like being out and suddenly suspecting I forgot to turn off the oven (a topic I wrote about, at length, in at least five issues of *Laughter and the Sound of Teacups*).

Laughter and the Sound of Teacups
February 23rd 2001

My pillow smelled like a huge lavender bag and one of my earplugs was lost. Sleep had been rather what my mother would term 'a production'. Lately it has not come too easily and I have an impressive regime of various aids to sleep, the lavender and the earplugs both being in that regime. The earplugs were more to block out the pervasive sounds of the girl downstairs' boyfriend's laugh, which carried on long into the night. I was waiting for them to stop talking to each other, start doing it and then pass out, but when the laughter showed no signs of being replaced by gasping I put the earplugs in. Bliss, all I could hear was the sound of my breathing and my jaws, rasping internal sounds. I had a number of dreams, all set on Enmore Rd, which I seemed doomed to traverse back and forth. At one point I was walking along the street holding three possums in hessian sacks, a grey men's suit and two sewing needles threaded with green cotton. The possums were what made it difficult, they kept squirming in the bags, trying to get out, and when they did I risked dropping the sewing needles, which I had balanced on top of the suit, instead of safely poked through some piece of fabric I was wearing, as in conscious life I would have done. I was taking the possums to a cafe that Tim owned, across the street from the RSL. When I walked in I was aghast to see that the floor was made out of girls' hair in ponytails. Immediately I felt frightened for my own hair, thinking he souvenired the hair of his patrons, indeed some long-haired girls were seated at a table looking nervous. Could he be the ponytail bandit, the man who I still fear will attack me with his scissors on public transport and take my hair as a trophy? I woke up before I found out. The telephone was ringing and I did my best job of answering it as if I hadn't been deeply asleep five seconds before.

I tried to sound perky, but I need not have worried, it was my mother. She was calling to ask me if I wanted to come to the bank with her later that afternoon and to ask advice about catching the bus. I realised she hadn't caught a bus for a very long time, not needing to with her car and the trains close by. It was still surprising to give instructions on how to catch the bus to the city, catching them almost every day myself, and in fact regarding them as vehicles operating for my own personal convenience rather than the public at large. The other people on the bus are only there to add some interest to my journey. Mother told me the story of how she had left the house she moved out of the day before, as I lay in my bed staring at the lines imprinted all over my body that looked like rivers and tributaries on a map. I could smell an unpleasant, beer-factory scent every now and again, and held the receiver away from my face as I made little sniffs, trying to detect the source of it. Mother was telling me how she left a note on the kitchen bench at the old house, wishing the new people a happy life in the house.

'I left some pink flowers in a little pot. People don't do that kind of thing anymore,' she said. I must have got my penchant for writing notes from my mother, as well as a lot of other things: distrust of my neighbours, an irreverent imagination and a tendency to giggle to name a few.

'It nearly polished me off, moving,' she said, 'I was carrying this big box along the footpath, to the house, when I tripped and fell over. I sat on the pavement with my box, so tired, not wanting to move. I sat there for a long time, thinking I could quite easily fall asleep with the box beside me.' I had heard the box story about three times already, but didn't mind hearing it again. Sometimes, you just don't want to get up again when you fall over. However in public places there is always some good Samaritan who wants to help you stand up. If you complain, protest that you want to rest on the pavement with your box, well, it's the asylum for you.

I said I would most probably come to the bank with her later, but I had to go and order my miracle elixir from the health-food store. 'Oh, I've already enquired about that,' Mother said, 'they don't have it.' Despite her enquiries she had the name of it wrong, and that is why they said they didn't have it. I had felt quite adult ringing up the health-food store and discussing ordering my miracle elixir, little did I know my mother had probably rung that morning. I think she gets frustrated because I am hasty to indulge my whims and yet slow to fulfill important obligations, especially regarding my health. When I hung up the phone I got out of bed and walked around wondering why my ankles and knees ached. The only possible explanation I could think of was all the walking I had done in my dream. I refuse to think that it is the ageing process, though lately I have been aware that my body is more easily strained than it used to be. My muscles seem too ready to ache.

I made myself toast and coffee and began to plan a complaint letter to Red Robin socks in my head. I turned on the computer, all set to type it out when I realised it would be better if I hand-wrote it. Typing it out seemed a little too organised and less impassioned than hand-writing, and since my writing is about as neat as when I first learnt to write I went looking for some sensible lined notepaper. I got it and the pen all ready before realising that I had left the article in question, the unsatisfactory socks, in my bedroom. Upon fossicking through my underwear drawer for them I again smelled the beer-factory scent, and walked around my room making little sniffs like a tracker dog, though they more snuffle than sniff, I suppose. After a few minutes I discovered the cup with the festering teabag in it that was the cause of the problem, and took it and the socks with me into the kitchen. I disposed of the teabag, thankful it was only that and not some other rotting dead thing that was decaying and causing the smell. I was shamefully mindful of the quarter of a piece of toast I dropped behind my bed months ago, that I was too lazy to retrieve and has been fodder for numerous late-night fears about what it could be feeding. This was usually a rat or mouse, but in other more creative moods it ranged to a snake, a horrible Cyclops-like worm-thing that I invented, and furry things with big teeth. I sat down at my desk and stretched one sock out in front of me, put the other on my right leg, and got out my ruler.

Dear Red Robin, I wrote:

> *I recently purchased a pair of Red Robin black knee-socks from Grace Bros (Macquarie Centre store). Upon trying them when I got home I was disappointed to note that they were far too short, in fact they are not what I would call knee-socks at all, ending about 8 cm down from the lower part of my knee. I am of an average height and weight (Shoe-size 9), and have average sized legs and would have expected the socks to be much longer, or at least stretchier so they could be pulled up.*
>
> *As it stands I can't wear these socks and have bought another brand (Sock Shop) which, though a little more expensive, fit much better, and actually reach my knees. I have enclosed the pair of Red Robin socks I found unsatisfactory and would appreciate it if you could refund my money. Thank you, Vanessa Berry.*

Take that Red Robin! I like writing complaint letters. I always manage to put in some sentence that makes me laugh, this time it was the one about the average-sized legs. It is true though, the socks were really short and upset me greatly, if I spend ten dollars on a pair of black socks I expect them to be long enough. I packaged the socks and the letter in a large envelope and sealed it. On the inside of the socks label there was a form to fill in if they were faulty, and at the top it said to send the *laundered* socks back. Similar to how in the information pamphlets you get with condoms it says, 'Should this product not meet your expectations, please return *unused* contents ...'. Yuck. I put the complaint letter in my bag, ready for posting and slowly got ready to leave the house. In the bathroom I managed to drop my pretty aqua hair band in the toilet, and I sighed as I watched it sink and settle. There's a certain feeling you get when you drop something in the toilet, just for a second you consider getting it out, but then shudder and leave it. It always upsets Matt greatly when he drops something in, he yells a heartbreaking 'Oh noooo', and I know exactly what has happened.

I dressed in beige and put my things in the bag I found in a bin in Waverton which smells like crushed cigarettes. Whenever I get compliments about it, which I do more than I would expect, I say 'I found it in a bin!' really proudly and wait for the reaction. Then I judge the person or people by their reaction/s. Matt had forgotten the leftovers he had intended to take to work so I put the plastic container in my bag, thinking I could eat it in a park somewhere and pretend I was on a lunch break. I rang him before I left the house, and when he put me on hold I was incredulous that I heard Elton John doing 'Lucy in the Sky with Diamonds'. It was terrible, not even funny. I looked for my sunglasses, checked my pimples and listened carefully to detect whether downstairs was clear of people so I could leave without being observed. Nothing worse than having to say hello when you don't want to. There was no one outside, only Dinner, who was sleeping in the sun. Dinner is the cat that the people downstairs have claimed, except they call it Moonlight, a far worse name for a cat than the one I gave it, which I happen to think is quite inspired.

'Hello Dinner' I said loudly and walked up the laneway as slowly as I could, for no reason other than I like walking slow. I increased my pace as I got in view of people on the main street, not wanting to be ridiculed. I caught a bus straight away, and was sitting towards the back, peacefully looking out the window when I felt someone sit next to me. There were heaps of spare seats and as we were approaching a stop I figured someone had got up and was just sitting next to me for a second, until the doors opened and they could get up and get out. I turned my head to look at the person who was mumbling 'sorry' (for bumping me, I suppose). It was a man in a green singlet and blue Stubbies, with a grey mullet, faded tattoos on his arms and a saggy old backpack with the end of a tennis racket poking out of it. He also smelled rather strongly of alcohol. I realised that I was the chosen one, he had chosen me to talk to out of everyone else.

'Are you having a good day?' he slurred.

'Not bad,' I replied.

'What does that mean?' he said. 'You having a bad day?'

'No, nothing has happened yet to distinguish this day as a good or a bad one, yet,' I explained, patiently and clearly. He didn't understand and I persisted, 'I'm only leaving the house now, something wonderful could happen to me while I am out, conversely something terrible could happen. I don't know. Nothing outstanding could happen, and then the most truthful thing I can say about my day is that it has not been bad.'

I always get myself into trouble by not reducing myself down to their level, the drunk-idiot level. He kept mumbling things at me, and when I didn't hear what he said I said 'I'm sorry?' until he raised his voice to tell me not to apologise.

'Luv, you don't need to apologise!' I don't know what he thought I was apologising for.

'Are you going to play tennis?' I asked, even though he was hardly in a fit state to walk straight, judging by his boozy scent and slurred speech.

'Nah, I already played.'

'Did you win?'

'No. But stop, I'm asking you the questions, you don't ask me questions. So have you had a good week?' It went on like this for a while and I refused to answer. He tried a new tactic.

'You've got lovely hands. I bet no one else has told you that.' As a matter of fact people had, I remember when I was at school my friends used to like squeezing my hands because they are very soft, fleshy and well kept. I didn't explain this to the man. He asked me if I change my nail polish every day, and why I was wearing a ring. When I said my mother bought it for me when I was fifteen he changed the subject quite quickly, I know not why, saying,

'You look like you've given up on yourself.'

'Well no, I haven't,' I replied.

'Good, good, never give up on yourself. Stop looking so sad, you're beautiful and young' and so on. 'Where are you going now?' he asked.

'The health-food store,' I said.

'Health-food store,' he said mockingly. I think he was trying to make fun of the way I pronounce my words properly.

'Health-food store,' he mocked again.

'Yes, the health-food store,' I replied, pressing the stop button. 'Excuse me please,' I said, clambering over his limbs and tennis racquet. 'Good day' I said, not looking back. I was thankful for my freedom. I couldn't understand half of the things he was saying in that alcoholic mumble, and his intention for speaking to me was not clear. There is something about me that attracts drunk old men. Or not even old men, just ugly ones with something not right up top. It is because I look sad most of the time, and they think something is wrong with me, that something terrible has happened to me or I am upset, when I am merely going about my daily business. I just have a sad face, and am disposed to melancholy in times of solitude. My other problem is the fact that I attempt to explain in my own words why there is nothing wrong with me, and why I don't want to lie and say I've had a good day when in fact good days are rarer than days that have few distinguishing features, good or bad.

This really gets them going. It is hard to argue to strangers, especially drunk strangers, that the aim of my life is not to be happy all the time, that it is, in fact, to honestly explore things within myself, and accept sadness and happiness as they both come, and enjoy them both for what they are. Drunk, ugly, crazy men, trying to make me look happy. Poor bastards. I looked at my watch: 12.30. Quite early to be offensively drunk, I figured he had possibly moved on to some other hapless person on the bus in my absence to spread his inspiring life message to them.

I sought out Vicky, who I had spoken to on the phone, in the health-food store, and she wrote down my details and we exchanged amazement at just how expensive one bottle of herbs can be. I put a deposit on it, a procedure which thoroughly confused the girl at the checkout, to whom I said, 'Maybe you should ask how to do it' which, later, I thought was quite rude of me. I was anxious to get to the park and eat my lunch and be quiet, as an antidote to my encounter with the drunk tennis guy. I bought a bottle of green Fanta from the kebab store, averting my eyes from the rotating glistening meat spires, and walked across to Victoria Park. The first thing I noticed was a couple of copulating ducks, but all was quite pleasant once I selected a spot under a tree, out of view of them. I set out my picnic, the plastic tub of food, a plastic fork I brought from home, the drink and a copy of *Little House on the Prairie*, my current reading material. I was up to the chapter 'A Roof and a Floor'. When I was in primary school I read the whole series of these books carefully and seriously, just in case one day I had to draw on the knowledge of how to build a log cabin. I used to make up extra stories using the characters and liked to call myself Laura like the girl in the book. From this I built up a complete alter ego for myself, and would make up fantastic stories about the various adventures Laura got up to. She was more confident than me and had better clothes. I ate my lunch as I read the chapter, I like eating and reading in parks, you can drop as much food as you please, it just gets hidden in the grass, so you can fully concentrate on reading. I read: 'They were all happy that night. The fire on the hearth was pleasant, for on the High Prairie even the summer nights were cool. The red-checked cloth was on the table, the little china woman glimmered on the mantel-shelf, and the new floor was golden in the flickering firelight', feeling very replete as if I were in the log cabin. I looked up when I heard shouting.

I realised the shouting had been going on for a while, gradually getting closer and louder. People nearby were looking around, as was I, until a woman wearing a ragged bra and a pair of jeans came walking down one of the paths, muttering viciously. At a distance of about fifty metres a man followed her, yelling 'Put it on ya dopey slut!' (I realised she was carrying a shirt in one hand) and then, when that got no reply he started to yell to everyone in the park, 'Look at the slut! Look at the slut! Whore!' and other worse things. The woman walked onwards ignoring him and crossed over the main road with him following after, still yelling. From *Little House on the Prairie* to that! I closed the book and observed the park. Inside the metal cage that fences in the pool I could see people sunbaking close together on the small rectangle of grass. In the park uni students sat on benches, kids poked the reeds in the pond with big sticks, and a man was standing very close to the tree I was sitting nearest to. I looked closely thinking 'oh, no, surely he's not ... not another one,' but thankfully he wasn't relieving himself, he was carefully setting up a camera and lining up a photograph. Damp-haired people strolled from the pool entrance to the bus stop, and a kid nearby was chasing seagulls. A hornet started to buzz around me and the remains of my picnic and I made a loud 'eek!' noise and moved sharply away, disturbing the man with the camera. He didn't look at me though, if he had I would have pointed and said 'hornet', to explain. Over the other side of the pond I could see a large pile of yellow and brown plastic bread trays, and packed up my belongings to go and investigate them. On the way I became distracted by the sight of tents on the lawn at Sydney Uni. I realised that it was Orientation Week, and decided to go and have a look, thinking I could score some free sweeties to have for dessert.

I joined the steady stream of students walking up the hill towards the main part of the uni. I could see a big sign that said 'Student Life' with the 't' of student enlarged and made to look like a Christian cross. Under the sign was a semi circle of plastic lawn chairs, empty. So that is what student life is all about, I thought, empty lawn furniture, compelling. As I walked around the various societies' stalls I noticed a distinct lack of originality regarding the free treats. About sixty per cent of the stalls had Chupa Chups, and the rest had some other kind of lolly, like jelly beans. It doesn't really add to the attraction of your society when you have the same lolly as every other stall. I was given a black and white cookie by the Bah'ai society, but neglected to pick up any other kind of sweet. As I walked along a tall boy approached me with a handful of papers.

'Would you like some information about the library?' he asked in a monotone. I looked at him – he resembled a very tall version of William Reid from the Jesus and Mary Chain, even down to the sunglasses. He was all in black as well. For half a minute I considered attempting to chat him up, but lost my nerve and merely said 'no thank you' politely, to which he wandered off looking aloof. I walked past the Asian Christians, the Madrigal Society, the Drama Society, the Social Skiers, the Korean Friends, the Pagan society and the Chess society. The great thing was that the people sitting behind these stalls guarding the Chupa Chups looked exactly as I expected them to look. The Pagan Society stall was manned by a fellow who had a beard and wild hair and a black shirt and some kind of silver amulet around his neck, the Social Skiers all looked freshly polished out of private school and the Madrigal Society had girls with long hair and slightly pudgy guys as members. Behind the Chess Society stall was a section of lawn set out with chess boards, and behind that, a large piece of canvas on the ground covered with painted hand-prints. William Reid wandered past me again, having no luck handing out his flyers. I went looking for the stall with all the drug information pamphlets on it, and the information about safe sex and counselling and all that. To my disappointment it had been scaled down from when I last went to Orientation Week five years ago, there weren't big bowls full of free condoms anymore, and no one was buzzing around with a bowl saying 'Would you like some free lube?' It was very disappointing. I went and sat and watched what was happening on the makeshift stage, on my way passing guys in fancy shirts who had a bowling lane set up with pins and bowling balls. How much I would have liked to ask if I could have a go, casually get a strike, and walk away to mutters of, 'Wow that girl is good!' I didn't trust myself though, being a patchy bowler, and confined that little scene to my imagination.

'Presenting LebSoc dancing for us today!' came an enthusiastic voice over the PA. I sat down to watch an embarrassed group of guys and girls dance half heartedly to Lebanese music. They looked like they were bored at a bad nightclub. They kept giggling and talking to one another. They were soon replaced with a display of Falun Gong, which had a cassette soundtrack of music and a voice speaking in Chinese. From what I ascertained, all it involves is standing straight with your eyes shut holding your arms out in front of your face for as long as possible. A woman eagerly handed me a thick pamphlet about it as I watched, which I slipped into my bag. Watching people stand with their arms in front of them gets boring after a while and I got up and left, checking once more on William before I went on my way. He had disappeared, possibly back to the library. I left via the sports societies, which I hadn't looked at yet. My favourite was the American Football society which had a handmade sign on A4 paper taped to the front of their stall that said 'Cheerleaders Wanted'. I unwrapped my Bah'ai cookie and walked down to the bus stop, humming 'Pleasure and Pain' by the Divinyls.

The week before I had gone on a great search for records and had seen, in Enthusiasms, the 12" single of 'Pleasure and Pain'. At the time I told myself I didn't need it, but ever since then I could not stop thinking about it, and how much I wanted to listen to the song. I decided that it was best to go and buy it instead of thinking about it all the time, and waited with a bunch of students for the bus. They were in a group and I thwarted their seating plans by placing myself right in the middle of a few rows of empty seats, after which I felt a small mean note of triumph inside my chest. I stared out the window for most of the journey. When the bus was pulled up at the lights I watched a man breaking up the pavement with a jackhammer. Despite the noise it was quite interesting, and he was wearing the same earplugs as I wore to bed the night before. The window was open and I considered yelling that amazing coincidence out at him, before realising the folly of yelling at someone using a jackhammer and wearing earplugs. George St was seething with people when I got off the bus, and while I waited for the lights to change so I could cross I noticed a group of old people staring at my socks. I started to feel defensive. They were brown knee socks, perfectly presentable. I then realised in fact they were staring at the BMW that lay beyond my socks, and making some kind of joke about it. As I made a break for the other side of the road one of the old men yelled 'Get it in Grandma!' excitedly. I quickened my pace and shot back a look of disdain. Old people nowadays are wild.

I waited in a long queue for the ATM, behind people who seemed to want to make complicated transactions, and needed to put their cards in and out lots of times. When it was my turn I decided to show them how it should be done, and pressed the necessary buttons as quickly as possible. ('If only,' Matt likes to say, 'The machine worked as fast as you pressed the buttons, so people who did it really slowly would have to wait for longer.') I felt very superior as I quickly received my cash and account balance and was out the door in thirty seconds. I walked past the tram stop and the Chinese BBQ store, which I have decided is code for 'window display of the most repulsive looking food items'. There were baby chickens lined up along a metal pole, something that looked like jawbones, big swollen orange things with tentacles, and other weird offal-coloured mystery items.

In the record store I flipped quickly through the Australasian Rock section. I couldn't find the single of 'Pleasure and Pain', so had to settle for the album instead, which was a bit of overkill but at least I had the song. I also purchased the collected works of Hunters and Collectors, to continue the 80s Australian theme. The guy who works in Enthusiasms is so unfailingly enthusiastic I sometimes feel nervous approaching the counter but I did, of course, and exited the store humming 'Pleasure and Pain' and thinking of the guy who wrote to me from prison years ago. I didn't write back to him because he made all these strange emotional pleas which seemed creepy and inappropriate, but I remember at the end of the letter he asked if I had any pictures of Chrissie Amphlett could I please send them to him because 'she's my rock'n'roll darling'.

For a long time afterwards if I saw a picture of her I thought of the prison guy, and wondered if he had Chrissie pictures all over his wall.

I had to wait for the bus for a long time. It was dreadfully hot, boys were walking around with their shirts off, and I had to keep wiping the sweat from above my lip with the back of my hand. I looked in at the store next to the bus stop, which sells those cumbersome shoes with forbiddingly tall platform soles. It is only a very small store and I realised that at the back of it, behind a metal grille, was a woman sitting on a stool and a wall of cigarette packets. I craned my head up to the writing on the awning, hoping it said 'Shoe Store and Tobacconist' but it didn't. When the bus did come it was an air- conditioned one and I settled myself comfortably in a seat near the back and read the next chapter of *Little House on the Prairie*, 'Indians in the House'.

This chapter is an exciting one, because Laura sees Indians for the first time. The whole way through the book so far Laura keeps asking Pa 'When are we going to see Indians?', and in this chapter her curiosity is finally sated. Another reason why it is a good chapter is because it features a lot of Jack the bulldog. After Laura, Jack is my favourite character, though there is a place in my heart for all of them. Pa has gone away hunting and Jack has been chained up because he has to stay at home and guard the womenfolk. Jack is not happy even though Laura and Mary 'stroked Jack's smooth, brindled head and scratched around his ears, and told him how sorry they were that he must be chained. He licked their hands a little bit, but he was very sad and angry'. That's the thing about Jack, he seems far more than a dog, he is sensitive, intuitive, fiercely devoted, intelligent, and displays a full range of human emotions which are readily interpreted by the narrator. Jack is one of those *special* dogs. The type that nowadays save families from fires, leap at the throats of potential murderers who are masquerading as door to door salesmen, that kind of thing. The type of dog that gets awarded a bravery medal, and in the photograph in the paper with the medal looks uncannily aware of their good deeds. I finished the chapter a few stops before mine, just when we were going past the big warehouse that sells ugly bronze statues. It stocks a complete range of bronze lions, deer, boars, and eagles, as well as copies of various famous sculptures. I noticed a new arrival, just off the truck, a life-size rhinoceros. These statues are expensive and ugly and, at close range, frightening. I walk past them sometimes on the way to the post office and pat their bronze heads, turn over their price tags, and say 'My aren't you an ugly thing ...'.

When I got off the bus at my stop it waited there for about a minute after I walked away. Whenever the bus does that I become paranoid that I have dropped something on the way out, and I kept glancing back and did a quick inventory of my belongings. I dislike being so nervous that I have lost things, I imagine if I knew how frequently, while out, I checked I had my wallet and keys I would be quite ashamed. No one came running out of the bus waving something I had dropped and it drove on up the street and I crossed the road. I like to get my keys out when I am waiting to cross the road, as if I am really worried about my safety. I was once told a tip for deterring strange men at night when you are walking is to get out your keys and jangle them in your hand, to make them think you are almost home. Alternatively if they do spring for you, you can try and gouge out an eye with one of the keys. I think about that every time I get my keys out too early. Really I do it because it gives me something to do while waiting for the lights to change.

At home I decided to delay the listening of 'Pleasure and Pain' until I had done the washing up and various other menial tasks. It would be sweeter if I waited, plus it gave me incentive to clean up. Matt had washed the dishes the night before. As usual he had left the most challenging pans until last, then forgotten about them. He takes about forty minutes to wash a small amount of dishes, he puts them all in the water and then goes off and watches television or eats a bowl of cereal, with the dishcloth over one shoulder to indicate he is still on the job, and the dishes are merely 'soaking'. This quietly annoys me a little, as I like to get right in there and do them all at once, and not stop until everything is finished, even the most challenging pans. With my washing finished I took my paper bag of records into the front room and took out the album. 'What A Life!' by the Divinyls, 1985. I put the song on about six times until I had committed the whole thing to memory, all the vocal inflections and such, and stood on the couch and did a mighty performance of it, belting it out. The stereo was flashing up 'Max Sound' on its little display, the ornaments on top of the bookcase were shuddering. I remembered that even as a child I liked this song, which is worrying considering the content (an eight year old belting out 'Please don't ask me how I've been getting off'). I didn't know what it meant of course, I only knew it was in some way 'dirty'. I was quite a slow learner as far as all the dirty stuff went because I was shy and didn't have friends to let me in on such great secrets as what a lesbian was and how babies were made. When someone did inform me of the latter I must have been about six or so, and I was incredulous. I didn't believe it, I thought it sounded quite stupid and weird, and was sure they were lying. I must have found out sometime they weren't lying, but I can't remember if I was disappointed or not.

I studied the cover of 'What a Life!'. It sure was ugly. Chrissie wears this sort of army coat which she is holding open at the front so you can see she is wearing suspenders. Woah! She is wearing completely white makeup and is pouting with lips that look like an oversized strawberry. On the back she is wearing a school uniform and is grabbing onto a wall and looking haggard. Next to her is a guy wielding a guitar in a classic rock pose, wearing exceedingly ugly clothing: tight pants with daggers on them, a leopard print pork pie hat and a shiny purple tapestry jacket. The rest of the band are hidden behind iron bars, possibly because they are too ugly. I like Chrissie, she always seems kind of bothered, *sexually* bothered. After my exertion (singing) I lay down on the mattress to recover, thinking my mother should have rung me by now to organise going to the bank. I stared at the old comics section from a Sunday paper that was beside my head. So many people I know leap for the comics section of the paper, but I always find it exceedingly dull and not funny in the slightest. When I was a kid I thought the comics were dull as well, but I liked the competitions where you coloured in pictures and won six dollars or some kind of prize. If you added glitter you were pretty well guaranteed to win. I remember being disappointed in them being so easily impressed and thought if I was judging it I would do it on artistic merit, rather than use of glitter. This issue was important to Fiona and I, when we were colouring we'd discuss how easy it was to win, and all our tactics. The best thing about the 'Funday Club' section this time was the quote I had written down on it, which I had overheard Matt saying on the telephone: 'The only reason she was appointed was because you said she looked pretty wearing a helmet.'

I got up and stared in the mirror and looked at my watch and said slowly, 'I've been stood up by my own mother'. I felt lonely and went to lie down again. After a while Mother called and told me to be ready outside, waiting for her to pick me up. Spirits enlivened, I quickly donned my shoes and went downstairs. I sat on the step waiting as Dinner sidled around my arms and back, butting her black and white head into me and making little noises. I didn't have to wait long before my mother appeared beckoning towards her car which was parked at the top of the street. She pointed to her crooked parking and said 'BAD' in a stern voice. In the car she showed me the cheque we were going to bank. It was the money she received for the sale of her house and it was a grand sum. I had never seen a cheque for so much, I held it on my lap the whole way. It was in a normal white envelope, which I thought was far too common for such a thing, it needed its own gilt lined box. Once we got moving I asked Mother how her attempt at the bus had gone.

'Horrible!' she said, 'it was so slow! It kept stopping and I had to sit right behind the driver and kept having to ask where we were. I won't be doing that again in a hurry.'

'Mum, it's a bus, of course it is going to keep stopping,' I tried to reason.

'And it wasn't air-conditioned,' she continued. 'You told me buses were air- conditioned.' I said about a third of them were, and that she would get used to catching buses. She did not look convinced. I remember not liking buses much when I first started catching them a lot, but if you know where you are going and when to push the stop button it is alright. I changed the subject to the drunk guy on the bus, and when I started to say how you can't look happy all the time Mother started violently nodding. She looked affronted and said the bus driver should have been looking out for me, and ejected the man from the bus. I argued that he was concentrating on driving the bus and there was no loud coarse language or violence or screaming to alert him. For all he knew we could have been old mates.

We were driving to the hospital where Mother works, to go to the bank there, because she liked the staff at that branch. We were served by Martin the Manager, a sprightly man with pale, fat hands and long almond-shaped blue eyes. He was a jovial fellow who spoke surprisingly casually to Mother. While they were talking bank I walked out into the antiseptic-scented corridors, but not too far because it is easy to get lost. I passed the sign to the dental clinic, then a little girl with stick legs in a wheelchair being pushed along by her mother. They were lost and I quickly escaped from the area they were in, not being able to help. I don't like admitting that I don't know where I am, merely a tourist among suffering! Back in the bank Martin was telling my mother how much he enjoyed calculating the interest per day on her new account, and I watched one of the tellers loading up the ATM with a huge pile of fifty and twenty dollar notes. It was compelling. She slotted them in and then the machine sorted them with a chewing sound, as she loaded the blank receipts into another part of the machine. She saw me looking and I turned away, nervous that I had seen something I should not have.

Instead I paid attention to the Australian Life Tables on the wall, which had graphs for the likelihood of people at ages thirty, forty, fifty and sixty to die of heart attacks, cancer and stroke. It was macabre, a perky bar graph in different colours for different modes of death, and then a column for the total likelihood of death. It was making me shiver, I turned back to Martin and Mother, who were talking about renovating bank branches.

'They won't give us money to renovate,' he was saying, 'it costs about $1.1 million to do up a branch.'

'Ooh!' said Mother, 'Vanessa and I will do it for half that!' I tried to picture how we would renovate the bank. Ideas were coming thick and fast mostly along the lines of Kitschbank, making it a museum of kitsch items as well as a bank! I didn't present Martin with the idea, in truth I was a little afraid of him. All I did was smile and nod when Mother said something I was beholden to acknowledge. After they finished chatting we left.

'Oh hurry up' Mother said in annoyance at the car in front of us, which had a wheelchair in the back.

'Mother!' I scolded, 'They were probably in a car accident and that is why they have a wheelchair!' She started to giggle. On the journey home we talked about what my sister and I were like as children, one of our favourite topics. Specifically our behaviour at school, how Fiona was feisty and defiant in primary school and I was quiet and never got in trouble. I worked out early that I far preferred to listen to what everyone was saying and store it in my mind for later reference, and to get revenge silently, using my wits. My biggest grudge was against Miss Marie, a sport teacher who routinely ridiculed me in class by calling me useless and drawing attention to how lazy and uncoordinated I was. I was so scared of her I often stayed home from school. Mother was instrumental in her removal. In a grand twist of fate I got to present a bouquet to her when she left (it was made like she was just leaving, although I knew the truth, Mother had told me that there had been a number of complaints about her, and she was suffering from *mental problems*. I told no one else this secret, not liking anyone particularly much) a fact which delights Mother to this day.

'Vanessa, would you study science?' she suddenly asked as we drove over the Harbour Bridge.

'Well yes I suppose so. I like science,' I said, to which she looked content and asked me no more about it. She told me about coming home from university on the train with her dissection kit and how the tail of the rat she was dissecting was hanging out from the side. She wondered why the North Shore lady across from her looked shocked and then she looked down to see ratty's long thick tail. This story is a classic, as good as *Little House on the Prairie*.

'Do you want to come back to my house for five minutes and try on the socks?' she asked. I had told her of my problem with the Red Robin and she had, of course, gone out to find me some proper socks. I declined her offer, I felt tired and hot and wanted to get home. As we waited at the lights near Wentworth Park Mother squealed in delight, seeing five small identical trucks in a row. They were advertising trucks, with big ads for Corona beer on the back.

'Look!' said Mother, 'They're all the same the cute little things!'

When we drove away I asked her what the ad had been for, as a test.

'Corona,' she said.

'Corona what?' I persisted.

'Oh, I don't know, its a kind of toilet isn't it?' she replied. I informed her that it was in fact a beer, and she nodded, not listening, still thinking about the little identical trucks. I wondered what would happen if the string of trucks got separated, say one of them got caught at the lights or something. They must have a radio link between them, I thought, so they can stick together at all times. I think advertising cars are environmentally irresponsible. Advertisement toilet paper is a much better idea. I think it would be a really viable idea, although probably equally as environmentally unfriendly.

It was bottle-shop rush hour on my street, being about half-past five. Cars were double parked in front of it, people were carting off cases of beer on their shoulders, the road became an obstacle course of people buying their Friday night booze. I got out of the car outside my house, took the ten dollars Mother waved at me and went inside to see what Matt was doing. He was watching the Channel Ten news, which is the best news because it is an hour long and thus has much more time to slot in the frivolous stories, like the dog Mardi Gras in some town in America, or a man growing a huge pumpkin. The best news story today informed us that a large French naval ship had pulled into Sydney, and over four hundred French sailors were out on the town, in their uniforms! At the end when it cut back to the newsreader he said 'ooh la la' in what I suppose was meant to be a sexy way, but in fact it was stupid and nauseating. Seeing a middle-aged man saying 'ooh la la' and popping his eyebrows up and down is highly unpleasant. The weather report came on, with Tim Bailey the wacky weatherman, who Matt has a passionate hatred of. He pounded his right fist into his left palm saying 'I *hate* him'. Every day Tim Bailey is in a new location.

Today he was at a beach with a group of disabled surfers, who were having a gala day soon. He introduced his 'good mate' Sticks, the disabled surfer, who (can you guess why he was called Sticks?) walked with crutches. He also introduced us to their mascot, Gemma the dog, a fat, blue cattle dog wearing a Disabled Surfers T-shirt. Then he did a perky wrap up of the weekend's weather. I don't like it when the weather person apologises for the rain. Everyone knows it has nothing to do with them and it shows they are getting a bit cocky; just because they read out the weather report they think they control the weather. He didn't let Sticks read out any of the weather report, or introduce us to any of the other disabled surfers. Sticks should have whacked him one with one of his crutches. I told Matt this. 'Yeah, take *that* Tim Bailey,' he said excitedly.

After the news was over I got Matt to help me fill in the form for the electronic rooster I am ordering from Bright Life products. This catalogue is full of the best stuff, my favourite being the rooster that senses someone walking past and greets them with a chirpy 'Cock a doodle do'. I have become obsessed with the rooster, making up little songs about it, the most pervasive being an adapted version of 'Zebra' by the Magnetic Fields: 'I want a roost-ahhhhhh!' I sing grandly. Matt finds it easier not to contest such dreams. He flicked through the catalogue to see if there was anything he wanted to buy, because he felt left out, but there was nothing.

After the form was carefully filled in with block letters I made myself a sandwich and went to listen to 'Pleasure and Pain' again. As I did the needle fell out of the stylus, which made me wail and cry about how the record player was 'ruined forever'. I tried to fix it for about fifteen minutes, with Matt hovering around saying 'Let me try'. I made a huge fuss about how nothing anyone could do would be able to fix it and stormed off to my bed where I lay face down, snorting in frustration. I waited for Matt to yell 'I've fixed it'. I have found the more I make a fool of myself getting upset and angry the greater the chance of everything being alright again, so I let myself go: wailing, screaming, hammering fists, threats of harm to myself and others, stomping, and so on. As predicted Matt fixed it in about two minutes, merrily oblivious to all my dramatics.

I could hear the television from the other room, a scandal show about prostitutes on residential streets, exploding gas heaters, the world full of disaster. My hissy fit had really taken it out of me and I was exhausted, I shut the door and closed my eyes, hoping to sleep. I could hear people yelling in the beer garden, excited drunken yells, and one woman in particular squealing loudly. I tried to think why she was making that noise. I decided it was probably some sexual joke she found really amusing, that is all such people laugh at. She was probably pretending to be really shocked and offended, just to draw attention to herself. What an unforgivable sin. Either that or she was being tickled, it wasn't a normal kind of squealing she was making, it was something that she could not control. I got sick of listening to it and got up and shut the window. The voices disappeared as soon as I shut it and I breathed a cinematic sigh of relief. As I lay down again I felt a twinge of panic that I was missing *Home and Away*, which was to be on in a few minutes, but then realised I didn't really care and fell asleep. I had a dream that I was writing an epic poem. This was how Coleridge wrote 'Kubla Khan', but unfortunately when I woke up I couldn't remember any of my epic poem, I was interrupted from my dream by Matt trying to find the pair of pants he wanted to wear to go out. I lay inert and unhelpful until he left. I heard his steps down the stairs and the slam of the door, and got up slowly and began to scuttle around the house. I have a habit of doing this when people leave, when I am hiding in my room I wait a minute then get up and start meddling with things, like a cockroach. Sometimes, also like a cockroach, when I hear someone at the door I scuttle off and hide, like they do when you turn the light on at night in the kitchen.

I made myself some dinner, planning on having it cooked just in time in order to watch the Grammies. I cooked tofu and green onions and dates and rice all together and carried a bowl of it out to the television. I missed the opening performance, which was Madonna, but got there just in time for the host to unleash a whole barrage of opening lame jokes. I had not watched an awards show for ages, because they are dull, and I never know who any of the performers are, and their jokes make me cringe. One thing I like about them though is when they put the camera on some star in the audience, and the star doesn't realise and is looking bored, or drugged. I didn't give it much of a chance. Performances by NSYNC and Destiny's Child failed to interest me. I hadn't heard of either of them before and my new knowledge was underwhelming. Paul Simon then came on stage and made a bit of a fool of himself by trying to be hip. Two guys then came out with this weird silver gun thing and fired t-shirts into the audience and got a huge laughing reaction. When it cut to the ad it previewed up-coming performances, all of which looked atrocious. I turned it off in disgust. They should really try and make them more interesting, somehow. Surely they know how painful the jokes are when they watch it over again later, or even while they are saying them. If I was up on stage coming out with such stinkers I would sure as hell be aware of it and try and be just a little more funny, or at least hurry along the proceedings a bit.

I made a list of things I could do:

- go and pick up a French sailor
- go across the laneway and talk to Drunk Man
- go watch Matt sing karaoke
- go to the city and walk around looking in bins to find discarded legal documents
- go to a restaurant and eat by myself
- watch the Grammies

I had a bath instead, which had all the appeal of sitting in a doctor's waiting room with no magazines. I even put bubble bath in it, but just sat in there glumly, after a minute thinking how bored I was, and how I wasn't even particularly dirty, and didn't need to have a bath. I decided I would get out of the water and put on comfortable clothes and get my sticky tape and stick Michael's letters back together. When I went to Strawberry Hills to check my post box the week before I looked through the bin of discarded mail and found a whole lot of letters to this guy called Michael. They were pen pal letters from women from different countries, with photos as well. He had ripped off the stamps and then ripped the letters in half and thrown them away! I don't think he even read them. I laid out all the pieces on the mattress and set about matching them up. I also turned on the Grammies again, because I could not help myself. Awards shows have this strange pull about them. I turned it on in time to see Dolly Parton, which was good, she was wearing a fancy white dress and looked great.

Michael's Forsaken Penpals.

Brilliant!

1. Kazumi, Japan.

Kazumi has sent Michael a number of letters and photographs, which all go along these lines: 'I'm thinking of you. My heart has been full of tender thoughts of you. My love for you will never change at all. I am praying for the day when we can meet again.' She also says 'I am very proud to have such a nice man like you as my sweet heart.' Little does she know!

2. May, Kenya.

There is a passport photograph of May clipped to the top of the letter, in which she looks sad. 'My family members are so happy about your planned visit. I told them that I'm expecting a special friend from Australia. When you come however you shall just meet my elder brother and sisters as both of my parents are dead ... I miss you dearly too Michael, and always wish that I could hear from you daily.' Ripped in half and in the bottom of the bin!

3. Katy, USA.

This was the first letter I got out of the bin. Katy is a bit of a saucy one.

'Michael, if I made a promise to you wouldn't you expect me to live up to it pretty promptly? Like for instance if I promised I would make love to you, how would you feel if I said I will live up to my promise ... eventually.' I read this and hollered to Matt 'I've struck GOLD!' and dug deeper into the bin. A woman collecting mail from her PO box looked at me and then walked quickly away. If she had asked I would have said earlier in the day I had mistakenly put an important piece of mail in there.

'What is Rock Melon? I've never heard of it. Oh, Apples with Peanut Butter is the bomb! (That means they're really great!)'

'That was so sweet of you to kiss my letter. Don't worry I won't ask you to put on some lipstick so I can see kisses either.'

In the words of our newsreader friend, ooh la la!

4. *Mami, Japan.*

'Hi! I send you my photo. It was taken on Bali last June. I'm ashamed a little because my face with no make-up. I hope you are not disappointment. See you again on net, Best regards, Mami.' The photo she sent is so good, she is really cute, sitting on a balcony with a piece of toast. Maybe I'll write to her.

5. *Jennifer, Smiley Rd, Las Vegas.*

'So honey have you ever been married? Any children? What do you do out there in Sydney??

For fun??'

Jennifer I will tell you what this guy does for fun – takes the innocent hearts of women the world over and rips them in two and stuffs them in the garbage! He also seems to collect postage stamps.

6. *Miki, Tokyo.*

He didn't even open this letter! It is really cute.

'Hi! How are you doing? I'm fine. I watched the Olympics on TV. I was so impressed with the opening ceremony. It was so wonderful and so cool!! The men riding the horses were so nice! I heard the mean what it's called but now I forgot its name. I think they were real farmer, weren't they? What are they called "Farmer" in there? I felt the Australia's culture during the opening ceremony. Your country is so nice!! But you are too busy to watch them, aren't you? I heard that you were so tired and sleepy everyday. It's poor thing!!,' and so on.

She encloses a photo of her and the kindergarten class she teaches: a row of exceedingly cute children, all wearing matching hats.

7. Angii, USA.

No letter but three perfumed photographs of a very dopey looking woman and kid. She is not a looker. Obviously not good enough for Michael.

I hate Michael. He is heartless. These poor women! I thought of writing to him myself, acting all sexy, making a place to meet and then standing him up. I would go along and secretly photograph him and make posters of his face that say 'Heartless' and stick them all around Sydney.

When I finished sticking the letters together I looked up and Eminem and Elton John were on screen performing a track together. At the end they gave each other a hug. Elton was wearing a hot pink and yellow polka-dotted suit. A man got up and gave a speech full of phrases like 'violence drenched society', 'the CNN of the inner city' and 'rap and hip hop delineate rite of passage, vicariously through music'. His mouth gobbled through big words like chewing Rice Bubbles. I flipped over to the ABC, which was showing *Love is a Four Letter Word*. Here Peter Fenton's character brushes his teeth. His girlfriend sits on the toilet saying, 'I'm trying to have a wee'. Peter finishes brushing his teeth and says 'I'll make you a hot toddy.' 'Say that again!' says the girlfriend in delight. 'I'll make you a hot toddy.' 'Ooh! I'm weeing! I'm weeing!' Gritty, cutting-edge television. Actually the episode wasn't too bad, mostly because it features a wounded pigeon as a main character, and Peter becomes obsessed with it, and talks to it. The pigeon bits were good and the twenty-something sexual dramas were kept to a minimum. By the end of the show I felt exhausted but watched *Rage* for a little while, though it was uninspiring. I can watch whole nights of terrible videos waiting for the next one, in the hope it will be good, it gets very hard to turn it off, just in case. After about an hour I pressed the off button on the remote control and the picture disappeared with a zap. I switched off all the lights in the house and felt my way down the hall into my room, and into bed.

Laughter and the Sound of Teacups
January 23rd 2002

The clock was far too loud, each second ticking off was as annoying as a dripping tap. The night before I had stared at it through the darkness in the unfamiliar room and thought about how I could pull it off the wall and smother it underneath one of the couch cushions. I hate loud clocks, I cannot even sleep wearing my watch, the ticking annoys me so much. I like to think it is because it confuses my heartbeat, but it is probably more guilt in being reminded of the passing of time, making me feel nervous that I am not using it to its best potential.

Early in the morning I heard noise from the kitchen, the night before Vic's aunt and uncle had got out of bed to welcome us when we arrived and Aunt Sheena had explained, 'We don't get up too early – quarter to seven', which I initially thought to be a joke but then realised was a serious comment. I woke up when I heard them in the kitchen and an itchy cough started rattling my chest. It had developed during the past few days, I felt as if I had a starfish of pain stretching out from my sternum, with pins along its legs sinking into my lungs, irritating them. I had a small cache of illness supplies next to the bed: water, tissues and cough mixture, and I reached down until I held the bottle of Robutussin DM 'Cough Control and Chest Congestion' and twisted the cap off between my index finger and thumb, before taking a swig from it and trying to get back to sleep. The cough mixture felt hot in my chest, I could feel it trickling down towards the source of the ache and the itch. I had already taken more than the recommended dose of it, something I often inadvertently do, out of frustration when a medicine does not work as well as I had hoped it would. This time it worked well enough to enable me to get back to sleep for a few more hours and when I woke up again I felt a bit better, I stared at the photographs on the opposite wall in a half asleep daze. I realised they were arranged in the shape of a crucifix, there were wedding photos from the marriages of each of Vic's three cousins belonging to this aunt and uncle, a graduation photo, and a photograph of three small grandchildren arranged in height order, one of those studio pictures that children and families get taken for posterity.

Below these photographs was an elaborate plastic doll's house, which Smith had played with for hours the night before. It made all these different noises, if you pressed on the dog and the cat they would woof and meow respectively, if you opened the back door you could hear the sound of birdies chirping in the garden, there was a computer which lit up when you touched it, a phone rung, the stove lit up, you could turn on the spa (waterless, but made a sort of bubbling sound) which was incongruously placed on the roof, and there was a large car with a row of buttons along the dashboard. When you pressed them they delivered various driving-related sentences in strong American accents. They had me howling with laughter, a male voice would say, 'Let's go eat' and then a female voice would say, 'Do we have the picnic basket?' then the man would say, 'Are we all buckled?' then a kid's voice would say, 'Let's go to the zoo!' The voices were stilted and electronic but very wholesome in tone. When

Smith realised that I found them funny he kept pressing the buttons over and over until it became annoying.

'You find this really funny,' he said, looking at me and releasing the words 'Buckle up!' from the electronic car.

'Sometimes, when you listen to something funny over and over it isn't funny any more, you get sick of it,' I explained to him. I like explaining things to Smith and usually I find myself explaining limits. I enjoy it, it reminds me that at the age of six anything seems possible – once something is funny, it always will be.

I heard Smith running around in the living room, a rapid thumping of feet drawing closer. He slid open the door to the room Tim and I were sleeping in and I knew he was standing in the doorway, wanting to play with the doll's house. Any second I expected to hear the car saying 'Let's go eat', but I must have been doing a good job of feigning sleep, because I heard the thumps of Smith's feet running off into the other end of the house. I turned over in the squeaky camp bed (to my horror it made an immodest creaking sound every time I moved. I dislike noisy beds, because if you are a restless sleeper, as I am, they make it sound like you are being obscenely active) and watched the hands of the noisy clock for a while, before deciding that I should get up and have a poke around the kitchen and make some coffee and food. I tried to get up as noiselessly as possible and not to trip over the doll's house, or the pram with the plastic doll in it that was parked beside the bed sheltering my cough mixture, or the edges of the video cassette cabinet, or the ends of the bed. So often I find myself running into the corners of furniture, as if I have some kind of eyesight problem, or perceive my body to be differently sized to how it actually is. I walk into doorframes as well, I am a bad judge of domestic distances. Today I didn't manage to run into anything, nor step on any of the dolls from the house (healthy looking specimens, two brown-haired males and two blonde females) and slid the door open quietly and peeked out into the house.

It was strange being there. Vic had invited Tim and me to come to Melbourne with him and Smith on Sunday afternoon, and we had left that night, in a rush. The trip had already been fraught with troubles and blots. This started when Vic lost his wallet, which had a thousand dollars in it, then when we were camping I suddenly developed the aforementioned cough and became worried about pneumonia. Despite this we decided to drive to Melbourne the long way, without a map. Because we didn't know where we were or exactly where we were going the trip took on a nightmarish aspect, time seemed to stretch out, we travelled down deserted roads through bushland, almost running out of petrol in a near ghost town inhabited by creepy country folk. Vic drove at frightening speeds that made Tim and me sick with worry, we felt lost, tired, poverty stricken and frustrated. The citizens of regional Victoria did not take kindly to us: a tall, thin man with lacy clothes and wild curling hair constantly looking for a payphone, a dour-faced girl with a hacking cough carrying a marrow, an eccentric six year old talking non stop and a worried looking fellow in the habit of striding off with a look of great purpose, a purpose unknown to anyone else.

We eventually reached Melbourne and were able to establish ourselves in Aunt Sheena and Uncle Iva's house. They were like the rest of Vic's relatives I have met, resolutely Scottish. Despite having lived in Australia for many years they still have strong accents, they start sentences with words like 'Och wee hen' and suchlike. Looking out into the living room and the kitchen my eyes skipped between maps of Scotland, photographs of castles and lochs, family crests, a tapestry of a Scottish piper, line drawings of a man in a kilt carrying a goat over his shoulders and one of an old woman with a sour face carrying a large basket on her back. The other presiding decorative element in the room was the Franklin Mint, there was a display case full of the kinds of dolls you see advertised on the back of magazines, in fact there were dolls in there I remembered exclaiming in horror over years before. 'Who would buy such a thing?' I remembered musing. There were a lot of baby dolls with wide pink mouths, one holding a hose, one covered with snowflakes, one playing with paint – I turned away so I didn't have to look at them. They looked eager like they were about to come alive and attack me, clamp onto my throat and not let go.

Smith was on one of the lounge chairs, wearing his pyjama top and underpants, sticking out one of his legs at right angles to his body and swinging it up and down. He started speaking as soon as I saw him.

'I got up first, you got up second, who do you think will get up next, then who will be the hairy chest?' he said in about three seconds. He has some kind of ruling that the last person to wake up has a hairy chest, which I do not understand the origins of. I had been the last up the day before, and since I had been dubbed 'the hairy chest' I tried to imagine what that would actually be like, and where the hair would be. I was glad that today the hairy chest would not be me again. With him talking in a fast, relentless stream I went into the kitchen and started to look around for the coffee-making devices and ingredients. Iva had shown me around the kitchen the night before in a basic way, but I was pleased to be able to find the things I had not been guided to – I am good at locating things in other people's kitchens. As I put the kettle on I watched Hamish, the twenty-year-old dog, shuffling blindly into the room where I had been sleeping, to get to his trampoline bed. I had shut the door so he wouldn't come in (Sheena told me that he 'thumps around a lot and keeps you awake' and that he had other places to sleep). He had a resigned look in his shuffle, as if he had been waiting all night for that moment, but was too tired to kick up a fuss about it. I was delighted by the fact that even the dog had a Scottish name, and amazed by its grand age, though perhaps a little dubious. 'He's almost in the Guinness Book of Records,' I said to Iva, who told me that the oldest dog age recorded is twenty-five. He had obviously been studying the subject, so perhaps it was true.

Tim got up as I was making the coffee, as did Vic, looking dishevelled – his hair sticking up messily, his eyes only half open, walking as if he was arthritic. I selected a mug for each of us, a brown one for Tim with stripes like a caramel sweet, a flowery one for Vic and one with the slogan 'God must have loved calories, he made so many of them' for myself. I had asked Vic if he wanted the mug with the 'World's Best Dad' cartoon on it, and he slowly shook his head and looked at me unamused. I like looking through the types of mugs my friends' relatives have. They inevitably include at least one slogan mug, or a star sign one, or one that makes some kind of joke about a diet. I like to think about how you could make a whole World's Best family with mugs, and how it is a strange thing to be reminded of when you are drinking a cup of coffee or tea. Oh, that's right (sip) I am the world's best daughter, along with the thousands of other world's best daughters using similar mugs.

Once the coffee was made and prepared according to our requirements I looked around for some breakfast food. I found the cupboard with the bread in it and the cupboard with the toaster in it. Vic's mother always puts the toaster in a cupboard after using it, it must be some kind of Scottish thing, or a family trait. There was a large jar of jam in the fridge, which must have been rather old, as some of the jam had crystallised. I tried to dig around the crunchy bits so there wouldn't be any on our slices, but when Tim asked 'Did you put sugar on this toast?' I realised I had failed. Vic couldn't eat his slice, he had some kind of tooth problem and could not chew very well or open his mouth very wide. He bit off one corner, made a face of great pain, then shook his head and pushed the plate away. Smith didn't eat his toast either, whenever I offer him food he says no, especially breakfast. The morning before I had been making cups of hotel granulated instant coffee and asked Smith if he wanted anything. He looked up at the saucer of sachets and said, 'Is that sugar? I want some sugar. I love sugar.' I looked over to Vic and asked him 'Can Smith eat sugar?' and he shook his head at me. 'No Smith, you can't eat sugar,' I said.

Vic had one of his hands on the side of his face and the other flipping through an address book, trying to find the phone number of his cousin who is a dentist. His idea was that the dentist cousin would treat him for free, and that would both solve his tooth problem and make it seem not so bad that he had lost a thousand dollars. After all, dentists are expensive. He embarked on a solid half hour of telephoning, which Tim and I made jokes about. He uses the phone more than anyone I know, and when he comes over to my house he always has a few calls to make, or has to check his messages at least twice.

'We should make Vic a coat of arms,' I said to Tim. 'It would have a telephone, a penny whistle, a suit ... the telephone cord could be wrapped around the penny whistle.'

'I hate being on the phone,' said Vic passionately, on hold from the childcare centre where his Aunt Betty works, 'I just have a lot of things to organise'.

After I finished my coffee I went outside to look at the back garden. As I had expected it was dotted with statues, birdbaths and gnomes peeking around the edges of neatly arranged plants. In the middle of the path Smith was sitting with his legs splayed out, smashing macadamia nuts with a hammer, then picking up the crushed remains of the nut inside and chewing on them. He had a look of great concentration on his face, and didn't even look up when I said, 'That's a much more exciting breakfast Smith.' I sat on one of the garden chairs for a while, and when I came back inside Vic was sitting beside the phone, looking defeated.

'What happened?' I asked, sensing that the dentist plan had not gone as expected.

'I rung up and I couldn't talk. I started to giggle and had to hang up,' he said. 'Tim made me ring back and they told me I had to wait for twelve weeks to get an appointment.'

With that out of the way we sat around deciding what to do. The next option, after visiting the dentist (Tim was going to go as well, he was excited about the idea of 'mates rates') was to visit another of Vic's cousins, who runs a donut factory.

'That freezer is full of donuts,' Vic said, pointing in its direction. The freezer was as big as the fridge and sat beside it like a twin. I opened the door to reveal drawers.

'Limbs, heads, torsos,' I started to joke, pointing to a drawer at a time. I like to make the predictable serial killer joke whenever somebody has a large freezer. I opened one of the drawers and there were dozens of donuts tied up in plastic bags. I started to have fantasies about the donut factory, but Vic seemed to think the donuts were made in the early hours of the morning, and he didn't look like he was about to start phoning up about the factory tour, so I busied myself by looking through my bag of hastily gathered clothes for something to wear. I collected my chosen clothing and the things I needed to have a shower and shuffled to the bathroom. I liked the bathroom, it was in the early stages of renovation, there were texta marks on the wall like the markings on bodies before surgery, and the paint on the ceiling had been stripped back to reveal all the old layers, one of which was a pleasant bright pink. There was a set of scales which I weighed myself on, which is always a surprise, I forget how much I weigh, and am bad at guessing – sixty-five kilograms. I thought about sixty-five bags of flour stacked up in a pleasant formation as I removed my sleeping-clothes, watching myself doing it in the full length mirror (another thing I do not have). I don't often look at myself naked, except for the occasional glimpse, and every time I do I am surprised by the fact that I am a lot smaller than I expect to be. It is not that I think I am physically bigger through any kind of worry about my weight, it is just that I feel so big in terms of emotion and thought, that sometimes it surprises me that I am not a giant-woman, I feel powerful and full of strong ideas and concepts and passion.

Encased in such a pale, small body, all things considered. I stopped looking at myself and drew back the sliding glass door to the shower. The walls were of the same design as the old wallpaper in my bathroom – when the old hot water heater was removed it exposed a mottled blue pattern which was also on these walls, although in green. The top ledges of the shower doors were lined with various bottles, which, when I reached up to grab the Anti-Stress Bathox, I managed to knock down with a great clatter. There were many bottles of Bathox, the poor man's Radox, which I believe does nothing whatsoever to relieve stress. Each of the different types (flavours, I was going to say, like ice-cream topping) promises a different kind of assistance – rejuvenation, relief. The anti-stress formula did not make me feel any calmer than I had before using it, and after washing it off me I'd had enough of the shower. I don't have great stamina for showers, in fact my average shower time would be about two minutes. I run out of things to do once I have made an effort to wash myself, I get bored just standing there. Perhaps in the future there will be e-showers, where the tiles are in fact a computer screen and you can send emails while getting clean. In fact, I might just pretend I have an e-shower, and begin my email messages with 'Guess what! I'm in the shower!' I investigated the progress of my blistered feet, which were looking a little better, although the skin around the blisters was marked with grubby stripes of band-aid adhesive. I have numerous small scars on my feet from wearing secondhand shoes and these newest blisters were infected and swollen to the size of twenty-cent pieces. I looked through the mirrored cupboard for band aids; I had a choice of assorted shapes, normal, or extra-wide varieties. I took two extra-wides and carefully put them over the affected areas, lamenting the state of my feet. I would like to have gloriously sexy feet but they are blocky, often grubby and often blistered, with weird thick nails on the little toes from the pressure of ill fitting shoes. I looked in the mirror and decided that though I was looking pasty and ill I would not bother hiding this under make-up, as often when I am feeling tired I like to rub at my eyes and my cheeks, and make-up prevents this satisfying act. I brushed my hair with the brush I had bought at a supermarket in Berry – I realised I had left mine at home, and having such long hair I need to brush it quite a lot or else it turns into a huge dreadlock which is painful to detangle. When I walked out of the supermarket carrying the brush Tim looked at me strangely and asked, 'Is that a hairbrush?' and I felt girly and took great pains to explain about knots and tangles.

I left the bathroom feeling somewhat restored and returned to the kitchen, where Vic had moved from his position next to the phone and was standing peering into the washing machine. He invited me to come out to the dryer with him and I followed him out to the shed in the back garden, which was full of useful clutter: fishing rods arranged along the roofbeams, tools hung up in rows on the wall. As Vic flung his clothes into the dryer I looked at the plum tree outside the door, with branches covered in clusters of purple fruit. Well I was pretty sure they were plums and therefore edible, but I have had bad experiences with picking fruit off trees thinking it's edible and then having to spit out a mouthful of bitter fruit flesh and worrying about whether I have been poisoned or not, so I picked one and merely rolled it around in my hand while I walked back to the house.

'Do you want to eat this?' I asked Tim, who was washing the breakfast dishes in the kitchen sink. He looked around at the proffered plum, which did not look particularly appetising when removed from its siblings on the branch, it looked small and unripe. He gave me an odd look and said no. I waited until he had finished washing and asked if he wanted me to show him the shed. This offer had more appeal and we went out into the garden, back to where I had been standing a few minutes earlier, with the dryer huffing out warm air and making a friendly rumbling sound. Smith pushed past my legs and stood in between us, watching Tim picking up a pair of red earmuffs and putting them over his head. He then picked up a sinister looking pitchfork which was trailing small spider webs and poked it at Smith, who giggled and twisted on the spot as Tim did a pantomime of spearing him on the prongs and eating him.

'I could eat your foot in one bite,' he said and Smith looked delighted. I thought back to the game I had played with Smith during the week where I tied a rope around his waist and dragged him along the floor, yelling about how I was going to sell him at the market. 'They do a fine trade in little boys,' I had threatened. Kids like fake storybook violence, though sometimes I stop and think: should I really be doing this? After the pitchfork pantomime was over I left the shed to investigate the cubby house. It had a sign 'Warning: Feral Children' hung over the door, and I stooped to enter through the small doorway. I was delighted to discover the cubby house fitted out with all sorts of miniature kitchen appliances and plastic food. There was a plastic chicken drumstick which Smith picked up and brandished at Tim, who was walking back towards the house. 'Eat this!' he yelled. I found a plastic fennel bulb, which seemed an obscure thing for a child to play with, or to have modelled in plastic. I inspected the plastic food for a while, and though I felt very safe in the cubby house I went back to the house to see if we were going to leave soon. There is only so much you can do in a house of people you do not know before you start to feel uncomfortable.

Inside, Vic was getting ready to leave and Smith was getting dressed, he had his trousers on back to front and his shirt unbuttoned and was tearing through the house kicking and yelling. I told Vic how Iva had explained the living-room carpet to me. It was not just a normal carpet, it was divided into squares so you could take them up and rearrange them, and redistribute them so the pile got even wear. The best feature was the fact you could remove them and hose them down, thus they were very easy to keep clean. 'This carpet is cleaner than any other,' Iva had told me, and I agreed that it was a great idea. I think I said something along the lines of 'Stains can be dealt with so easily!' in the excited, flattering way you speak to relatives when they are showing off features of their house. I realised the more I talked the longer it would take to leave, and I followed Tim out to the ute to give Vic some time to gather himself and his belongings ready for departure. Tim opened the back of the ute and a warm, sour smell escaped from it, a combination of campfires, dirty clothes, a bucket of dirty dishes and the sinister depths of the esky. I went around to the passenger door and looked in at the chaotic mixture of objects littered over the seats: the marrow and squash I'd bought from a roadside stall, pillows, empty soft drink bottles, scraps of paper Smith and I had been drawing on (I drew a dinosaur scene with a surprisingly skilful pterodactyl soaring above the land-bound dinosaurs, and also an alien scene with a tank and a riot policeman trying to apprehend the aliens, who were going on a spree of destruction, bouncing across suburbia on a platform with springs for legs. I had drawn a squashed house and a sad looking stick figure saying 'oh no' underneath this bouncing platform) and other assorted pieces of trash. When I went back in the house Vic was ready so we left, making sure the house was properly locked according to the instructions Iva left written on the white board that began,

'Please ensure the back door is properly locked ...' Instructions on how to push in the button in the centre of the doorknob followed.

The whole time we were in Melbourne we did not manage to figure out what suburb we were staying in. I asked Vic numerous times because I don't like not knowing where I am, but he never did remember nor find out. We drove past small neat houses on regular sized blocks, down streets that already looked familiar from the few times we had travelled down them the day before. We drove past the small sign for the Joy of Music Piano Teacher, then the Mordialloc Gymnastics Club, into which a slow, jerky procession of old people was proceeding. Geriatric Gymnastics? I giggled quietly thinking about it, though I really had no right to, there are probably old people who are more gymnastic than I am, having never been able to do even a handstand, even when I was young and supple. We drove past a house painted bright yellow, the colour of the sun in children's picture books, which I noticed with delight as I have always thought that not enough people paint their houses garish colours. Near Mordialloc station someone had changed a sign to read 'Melbourne Slut Car Central', and I could not work out what 'Slut' could have possibly been changed from. We parked at the shops and I got some money out for Vic, which he tucked gravely into his top pocket, and we discussed the plan for later in the day, as Vic was going to visit his grandmother and Tim and I were going to the city. I felt sorry for Vic, his holiday seemed full of bad luck and unpleasant details: his Melbourne trip was to visit his gravely ill grandmother, he had lost all that money, we had got shirty at him because he was driving wildly over the speed limit, the soy milk in the esky had spilt out and coated everything inside it with a sour scum, he had spent at least thirty dollars using payphones to organise various things that seemed to be incredibly difficult and laboured.

We left him and Smith outside the 'Your Opportunity to Shop' op shop, which I exercised restraint in not visiting, although I could see a tempting $1 rack, and walked up to the train station. As I struggled with the ticket machine that would not eat my $20 note and told me to insert coins or smaller notes the railway crossing alarm started to clang violently, and I told Tim we should just get on the train and buy a ticket at Flinders St. As soon as we got on the train we were confronted by a sign that asked in large red letters 'Can I see your Ticket Please?' and then went on to detail the various penalties that could apply. I quickly sketched out an explanation in case we were apprehended by a ticket inspector and then thought no more of it. The seats on Melbourne trains are arranged so they are facing one another, unlike Sydney ones where you can move the seats to the direction the train is travelling, and there are very few seats where you are forced to sit facing other people. Luckily this train was not very crowded, so we didn't have to spend the journey trying to avoid the eyes of the people opposite. Tim stared out the window and I watched the teenagers at the other end of the carriage. They were talking for a while, then one of them lifted up his arms and the girl next to him sniffed his armpits. I figured he must have asked 'Do I smell?', and she was checking for him, but then she lifted up her arms and he did the same to her, and then she sniffed his again. I thought they must be comparing the scent of their deodorants, or else they had some kind of perspiration fetish. This sniffing went on for about a minute, then I became distracted from them by a group of freshly dressed skater girls who got on the train at Moorabbin. They were talking about this guy they know who they call 'Burnt'.

'Why do you call him that?' asked one of them.

'Coz he's hot!' the ringleader exclaimed and then went on to explain the connection between hot and burnt, which I thought that she could have perhaps let her friend work out for herself.

They were dressed so similarly that they reminded me of those puzzles where you have to look at a group of cartoon people or animals and read through the description of what the one you have to find is wearing, slowly eliminating details until you find the correct one. They had only minor differences. At least four were wearing baggy denim pants with chains looping out from the pocket, they had crisp t-shirts displaying cryptic slogans and a few of them had skateboards. A few stops after they got on more of their friends appeared and they began to compare their skateboards.

'I got a new one and I went out into the street and was banging it against the road to scratch it,' one of them said loudly. 'I hate it when things look all new.' I initially condemned this sentiment, but within a few seconds was accosted by a shameful memory of doing something similar with a new pair of Docs at the age of fourteen – walking through puddles, kicking brick walls, and so on. I listened to their conversation the whole way to the city, amazed at just how dull it was. I was sure I must have been more interesting when I was fifteen. They were discussing different shoe sizes, and how sometimes shoe sizes can differ depending on the brand of shoe. 'In these I'm a nine but I've got these other ones that are an eight,' was a typical comment. I turned back to see what Tim was doing and was surprised to see him waving out of the window at a guy in a flat opposite the train station who was looking out from behind a curtain. Not to be left out I waved as well, although I am not sure if the guy saw me. We discussed how he must be able to do that a lot, living right across from the station, and how nice it must be to be able to do so much waving to strangers. I love waving from public transport, it fills me with a particular kind of joy. The girls were now talking about the upcoming Big Day Out, and how they were going to get up early, listen to all the CDs, get 'pumped' and then get one of their dads to drive them to the venue just before the gates opened. This topic annoyed me and I felt very impatient, the city still seemed remote. When we had caught the train the day before there were so many stops that I began to wonder if we were going in the correct direction, there was no network map on the wall of the carriage, only stern reminders about fare evasion.

At South Yarra a guy got in and started to read one of the street press papers, which had a cover story about the Big Day Out. One of the girls got really excited about this and said 'Wow! Where did he get that!' as if street press was special and difficult to come by. At this point I turned away and joined Tim in staring out the window until we reached the city. The driver announced the few stations left to travel, beginning with 'Okay folks' as he had done with the other station announcements he had made along the way. It had taken me a few announcements to realise that was what he had actually said, it seemed too friendly for a train driver. I wondered just how free they can get with their announcing, and tried to imagine the style I would use for this – I was sure it would be both creative and amusing.

As soon as we got off the train I started to walk fast to get away from the girls, I could not stand their excitement any longer. The platform smelt of potato cakes, a rich greasy scent leaking from the station kiosk. We walked down into the tiled tunnel that leads to the underground station exit and the little arcade lined with odd shops. The tunnel reminds me of a giant drain or a giant bathroom of some kind, as does the arcade it leads on to. I like to imagine that I am actually walking in a drain that has been enhanced with retail outlets. I prepared myself to act charming to the station attendant, who was leaning over the ticket gates. I started to tell him how the ticket machine would not accept my money, and he pointed over to the newsagent and told us to get tickets from there. He was so unconcerned that I felt slightly disappointed, I had wanted him to make more of a fuss. In the newsagent I paused in front of the counter, undecided whether I should buy the tickets because the station man didn't look like he cared whether we bought them or not. Just to be safe I bought a couple of tickets and gave one to Tim and kept one for myself. We walked up to Sticky, the fabulous zine shop, and I asked the pleasant fellow behind the counter if I could get the money for my zines that had sold. He looked a bit worried and tapped away at his computer for a moment, before lamenting his incomplete records and asking me how many I had sent of a certain zine a few months earlier. As usual I had no idea and we decided, after some discussion, that he would give me twenty dollars and they would send me the rest. I was very glad of this, having spent a lot of money I could not really afford to spend in the past few days. I could not be stingy with Vic having lost all that money, begrudging buying an expensive skimpy plate of baked beans on toast in a country town cafe seemed very petty in the light of losing a thousand dollars. I looked around the store for a little bit, took one of the free zines which looked amusing and bid a cheery farewell to the guy working there.

We passed the tiny bookstore that is run by a man who also has the surname Berry. I like finding other Berrys with idiosyncratic concerns. The bookstore works on a system where the books are arranged behind a window with small cardboard price labels taped to the outside of the glass. If you want to buy a book you remove the price sticker and affix a note to it, slide it under the door and return when it is open to claim your book. I have never done this but am very fond of the method. After looking over the books in the windows we went in search of another bookshop, Collected Works, which we had spent half an hour searching for the previous day. It had moved from where Tim remembered it to be and after asking at a number of places, looking up phone books, and wandering up and down Flinders Lane at least three times we came to the right address, only to find it shut and the cops frisking some guy in the doorway. Today, though, we found it open. We went down the stairs, through the bead curtain and silently split up and began looking at the books. I settled down in front of the James Joyce section and began to flip through books about *Finnegan's Wake*. I felt self conscious doing this, but I spent so much energy, time, patience and concentration reading it three years ago that its completion remains one of my proudest literary achievements. Reading about the complicated decoding of it reminds me of that time in my life: it was summer, I was visiting every St Vincent de Paul op shop in Sydney and wearing uniforms and white knee socks every time I went out. After looking at these books for a while I moved on to the British section, where I sat cross-legged on the floor to look methodically through the shelves. When I am in a bookstore I tend to reach for the books which are familiar to me, or ones with good names, or authors with interesting names, or decide their worth solely based on the cover. Wrong, I know, but irresistible. I find that often you can judge a book by its cover, though the proverb tells me otherwise. I started to read an Anna Kavan book which I wanted to buy but could not afford, it was old and out of print and weathered looking. I read a whole story about a woman being released from hospital and then looked up to see what Tim was doing – studying a book in the Australian Fiction section with a serious expression.

A record of old, French music was being played in the corner, which suited the atmosphere of the shop well. It was neat but cluttered, a little dim, and dotted with quiet, studious looking customers with their heads bent over books. I looked at some poetry books for a while, until I found a phrase that I liked about streetlamps bent over like the heads of geese. I wanted to write it down but upon rustling through my bag I realised I didn't have a notebook with me. I dug through my bag until I found a biro and a receipt with a blank back, and awkwardly propped the book open to transcribe the line. My pen didn't work and no amount of scratching it against the paper or my arm would make it work. When I looked up I realised the woman behind the counter was staring at me, which made me blush bright red and quickly put the book back on the shelf and my paper and pen back in the bag.

I remembered that I promised to call Vic when I got to the city, so I decided to do that while recovering from my embarrassment. Tim gave me a roll of film with instructions to leave it at a one-hour photo place, but only a Kodak one, if I happened to pass such a store. I quickly brushed through the noisy bead curtain, convinced the woman behind the counter was staring at my back suspiciously, and looked at my reflection in the long mirror across from the entrance. Long mirrors seemed to be following me around, reminding me that I looked pasty and that my white T-shirt was verging on see-through. The phone at the top of the stairs was broken, so I crossed the street to the next closest one, which happened to be outside a Kodak one-hour photo developing shop. I was proud of myself for finding one so easily, and dropped the film off there, giving Tim's surname instead of my own (deciding which surname to leave inspired a minor mental crisis which was over in less than three seconds, though quite intense while it lasted). Getting photos developed in one hour is something I do rarely and when I do I feel kind of luxurious, knowing that I am put in priority over the people who feel they can wait a day for their obviously less important pictures. I took the receipt for the photos and went to the phone to call Vic at his grandmother's house. A Scottish voice answered and I asked to speak to him, and after a minor confused-sounding pause Vic picked up the phone, sounding weary.

'There are lots of people here,' he said quietly, which I took to mean that the atmosphere was tense. He gave me the phone number for his aunt and uncle's house and I promised to call him later in the afternoon. After I hung up I spied some of the teenage girls who had been on the train outside Coles, sitting around looking bored and a little mean. I was not surprised that they had come to the city to do such a thing. I went back to the bookstore and handed Tim the receipt for the photos and he looked up surprised, as if he had not actually expected me to find a photo shop. I then returned to the racks, flipping through a Margaret Atwood biography, trying to find the section where she was my age, to compare and contrast. At my age she was at university, not caring too much about her appearance, and writing poetry, three things that I am probably doing the opposite of. I had been hoping to discover an uncanny life parallel, meaning that I will develop into an esteemed novelist.

I was feeling too distracted to look at anything in depth, mostly because I was hungry. When I am hungry I feel acutely distressed and find it hard to pay attention to anything but the spirals of emptiness shooting through my guts.

'Tim, I have to go and get some food, you know how I get when I am hungry,' I whispered urgently. He nodded and I reassured him that just because I was hungry we didn't have to leave, he could keep looking, I was just in a state of distress and could not concentrate.

'I don't have any money, and there are too many tempting things,' I added.

'But it's just nice to look,' he replied, and I felt a bit ashamed that I had reduced the joy of looking through books to whether I could afford to possess them or not. I scurried out through the curtain again and tried to think of where I could get something small to nibble on. I walked past a newsagent and thought that perhaps I should buy a notebook to save me the indignity of having to write on the backs of receipts. The newsagent I entered, though, seemed only to sell greeting cards and lottery tickets, there was a long line of lunch break workers holding tickets in their hands, looking hopeful. From there I went to Coles, which was far too confusing and similarly busy, so I walked aimlessly out again and crossed the street to another newsagent which had a more extensive range. There was a choice between a small, plain white notebook and a spiral bound lined one, both for 50 cents. I am very particular about the style of notebooks I use, I have different preferred sizes for different types of writing. A palm-sized notebook for quick notes, writing down ideas, collecting phone numbers and addresses and writing to-do lists; thick old foolscap books for journal writing and sometimes story writing; lined loose-leaf foolscap or notepad A4 for long letters; and smaller pieces of miscellaneous paper for short letters. I prefer to write in black biro at all times. Of course these restrictions are not so deeply ingrained that I will not deviate from them, however they are my preferred methods. I chose the plain notebook – more scope for note-taking, I decided. On the way out I looked quickly through the reduced items box, but all that was in there were rolls of faded dark green streamers for 5 cents (I knew no one was going to buy them, I almost did because I felt sorry for them) and ugly photo albums.

My search for food was a desperate one. I walked through alleyways lined with cafes and cluttered with tables and stylishly dressed Melbourne citizens, but all the food at these places was somehow not right. I lined up at a fruit store for five minutes to buy an overpriced banana, but the line was moving too slowly and I dumped the banana back where it came from and went to the shop next door, which I had been too hesitant to enter when walking past beforehand. It was a health-food shop and upon entering it I said hello to the woman who I thought I had seen behind the counter earlier, although she was now sitting at one of the tables eating a plate of rice and vegetables. As soon as I said hello I was overcome by the fear that she was in fact just a customer, and my greeting made me look eager and desperate for human contact. To my relief she stood up and moved behind the counter and I bought a nori roll which she wrapped up in crackly, translucent paper. I started to eat it as soon as I was out of the store. I have finally got over my phobia of the ends of sushi rolls being like eyes and can now eat them again, although only one does little to quell insistent hunger. I finished eating it quickly and did my customary check with my tongue to feel if seaweed was adhered to my teeth. When I was satisfied that my glorious smile would not be ruined by shreds of dark green I went back to the bookstore, where Tim was still in the same place I had left him. I spared him the long tale of my search for food and looked through a book about Anne Sexton, which had copies of the letters and poems she wrote in the last year of her life. The most interesting pages were drafts of her poems typed out with thick, black ink corrections scrawled over the top of the words. I love to look at a page of edited typing, especially one that I have created myself, I feel so proud and industrious. I like to compare my own style with that of others, the different types of crossings out and arrows and abbreviations.

When we left Tim was pleased by the fact that he had spent almost two hours in there straight. Our next stop was the photo shop.

'Here you go Miss Wright,' the guy behind the counter said as he handed over the paper envelope. I felt a sense of satisfaction that he did not know my real name, that I had successfully managed to deceive him and Tim, waiting outside, was in fact the owner of that surname. After I left the photo store we went to one of the cafe alleyways to buy some coffee.

'The man in the store told me to look through the photos to check they were mine,' I said. 'I opened up the packet and flipped to one with Ryan's head in it, so I figured that they were yours.'

Tim was not so convinced. 'I didn't take any photos of Ryan, are you sure?' he said. To settle the matter he opened up the envelope and took out the photos. He was immediately disgusted at the poor-quality processing, and chastised both himself for being impatient, and the photo place for not taking adequate care. Each photo he turned to made him shake his head and make a disgusted clicking noise with his tongue. I started to feel somewhat responsible and looked quietly down into my coffee. The photos were of Coogee beach, from a night the week before when we had gone there to eat chips and walk along the path to Bronte. They looked beautiful, bright and warm and unearthly, and I remembered what a good, happy night it had been. As well as these there were some pictures of Ryan and me in my kitchen which made me vow to make more of an effort dressing and looking good at home because I was putty-faced in them. I tried to distract Tim's attention with the heart drawn in the froth on top of my coffee, but he was mumbling about shoddy workmanship. He did laugh at me spooning the froth into my mouth from the bottom of the cup, I was doing it avidly, the spoon scraping against the ceramic side of the coffee cup. With it all gone I went to pay, the girl behind the counter asking 'Just the coffees?' as if I was suddenly going to astound her with further orders.

Our next proposed stop was the black-and-white photo booth. We had been planning the various poses we could do – hands around each others throats, Tim strangling me with my plait, me pretending to cut off his ear with his pocket knife – but unfortunately there was a queue outside the booth. I noticed that it had gone up to four dollars since last weekend (the last time I had been in Melbourne) when it had been three, and felt mildly affronted at this price rise. We gave up on the murderous photo booth idea and crossed the street to catch the tram. On the back of the waiting tram was an ad for KFC's Popcorn Chicken, the repulsiveness of which we had been discussing a lot over the past few days. It featured an open mouth with a round grizzled up piece of chicken on the tongue, which looked moist and pink and horrible. I think the trend towards making fast food seem exciting and extreme is really odd; the food equivalent of extreme sports. If people are really after excitement and extremity in food they should just eat whole chillies or something. As we walked towards the tram I giggled at the strange grunting noises Tim was making in time to his footsteps, something to do with the warmth of the sun feeling good, he let on later. We got in the tram and he put his ticket in the validating machine. This action was a bit of a joke, the Melbourne public transport system appears full of loopholes, validating your ticket seems to serve no real purpose. He took it out again and looked at the back.

'The twenty third,' he groaned, thinking of the grunting noises he had just been making. 'I'm not going to talk for the rest of the day,' he said. 'No, I am going to start a rival publication – The Real Story – with all the things that you leave out. I'm going to put in all the embarrassing things you don't mention that you do.' I felt a little nervous, and began to defend my project in a half-arsed way, though this talk soon petered out and Tim began to read *Inpress* and I stared at the crook of my arm where a pimple had appeared right above the thick vein right in the centre. It was an unusual pimple location and I stared at it closely and poked at it for a while. After this became boring I smiled at the little girl sitting across from me a few times, hoping she would smile back (she did) and read the paper over Tim's shoulder until we were travelling down Sydney Rd. We both looked out the window and commented on how little the street had changed over the last few years, unlike Sydney, where whole streets are renovated to the point of being almost unrecognisable, the past feels either glossed over or erased. We got out at the stop just near Tabet's Bakery and I congratulated us on remembering the right stop.

'We are so ... good,' I announced proudly. Tabet's makes the best oregano pizzas, I have fantasies about them and every time I go to Melbourne I try to eat there at least once. We ordered pizza and coffee and sat at one of the tables discussing the food we had eaten on our first day of driving. It was a terrible list: porridge, half a vegie burger each, bread rolls, Chelsea bun, hot chips, bread with peanut butter on it, pistachio nuts, instant coffee, bread with tomato sauce on it, passionfruit fizzy drink and this stuff called cracker mix made up of dehydrated peas and pretzels. At the end of that day I felt bloated and heavy, like a giant walking pimple. We were both quiet after running through this list, feeling guilty and a bit ill. Pretty soon our pizzas were ready, all rolled up and wrapped in paper. As I ate I stared at the man behind the counter taking and fulfilling orders and the faded posters of sites of natural beauty in Lebanon on the walls. Although I tried to fool myself that I was still hungry and could eat another one I exercised restraint and went up to the counter to pay.

After we left Tabet's we walked up Sydney Rd towards Coburg. Tim used to live in Coburg and pointed out to me the places he used to frequent. First was a pub called Adrians with a window display of empty bottles of spirits, embedded among rocks.

'They had to put empty ones in, otherwise it would be too tempting,' he said. We walked past a sports centre that had a row of trampolines behind the windows. Through each window I could see a kid bouncing up and down happily.

'I know which was your favourite,' Tim said, 'the plump one.' I had to admit that, yes, the plump kid bouncing up and down smiling and wobbling had been the one I was most drawn to. We stared in at an empty pharmacy, which still had all the shelving and the pastel-painted fixtures and the signs for Prescriptions and Baby Care and other sections. It looked almost pretty, the shelves were clear plastic and, without stock, looked decorative. The empty pharmacy was on a corner, and Tim pointed down the cross street and told me that there was a milk bar that sold Coburg Cola in that direction. He had been looking out for Coburg Cola as we walked past the different stores, apparently it comes in a glass bottle and is very sweet and very local. We walked past many wedding photography stores and I wondered how it would feel to have a print of you enlarged and hung up in a window to advertise the photographer's services. I would like it, of course, though I doubt very much I will ever employ the services of a wedding photographer (do wedding photographers feel somewhat frustrated at their own weddings, itching to take photographs, or feeling every stage in terms of a different photo moment?). As we walked a couple approached Tim and one of them asked, with an English accent, where they could get a cup of coffee nearby. He was laughing as he said it, as if he was making some kind of joke, so Tim didn't reply. I and another girl passing by directed him to the many Lebanese bakeries and cafes.

'You're walking past all the best places to get coffee,' she said to him, a mite sternly. I looked back to see if they were going into one of these cafes, or whether the question about coffee had only been some kind of joke. They continued walking.

We entered an arcade so Tim could buy a pie and I went off to find the bathroom. I inched past the wet paint signs hung on the door and tiptoed in, hoping no painters would be in there to tell me off. There was no one, and I touched part of the wall to test it, to find it sticky with lemon coloured paint. The air had that toxic fresh paint smell and I felt light headed by the time I walked out again. Tim was sitting on a bench in the centre of the arcade, eating a seven vegetable pie. We tried to name all the vegetables that were in it but fell short by a couple. When the pie was finished we read the plaque on the wall that explained how in the 70s this arcade had been built on the site of an old store. This fact was obvious as every detail was redolent of that decade, from the vertically arranged bricks forming the interior wall, to the abstract, enamel tile mural, to the shop signs hanging down from the ceiling on thin poles. We listed the 70s features for a while, and did a little dramatic reconstruction of the public's reaction to the modern tile mural. After this we watched men carry crates of records into a half-constructed store for a while, both probably wishing we could go in and have a look through the boxes before anyone else got a chance to. When we left the arcade I remembered that there was a park nearby I had been to once and taken a very pleasant walk in. I was convinced that this park lay at the end of the street.

'What's at the end of this street?' I asked Tim, who looked at me blankly and said 'Sydney'. Sydney Rd, well of course. I blabbered out an explanation of how I thought it was a different street, and we turned off to look for the park in another direction. We walked through a grassed area next to some tennis courts, where a man was walking his dog, the idea being that the path might lead to the park. The path narrowed into an alleyway behind a row of houses, and at that moment I realised that no one knew where we were, a feeling I love. Nobody would be able to guess we were walking down this little path in Coburg. Few people even knew we were in Melbourne, besides Tim's mother who had called just before we left. I felt secret and concealed.

The path turned into a street running alongside more sporting fields. Tim ran off kicking a bottle with great aplomb and I read the teenage graffiti written on the wall, 'The Cult' and 'Class of `94' to which someone had added 'War' under 'Class'. 'Class War of `94' has a good ring to it. Someone had also written how much they hated one of their teachers, and I thought of this teacher walking her dog one day and being confronted by the message of how much she was hated by her students.

We went into the grid of suburban streets, noticing how quiet it was with only the faint sounds of far away traffic and birdies chirping, hidden in the trees. I told Tim about how, when I am walking through such an area, I like to think that I could knock on the door of one of the houses and ask to come in for a glass of lemonade or a cup of tea. Inside the house I would be shown all the best knick knacks, the ones locked up in the display cabinets, and told stories about the framed photographs lined up on the mantelpiece. Tim told me about a tour that was once run in Perth where a busload of people were taken out to the suburbs and shown around like they were in a new city. Examples of typical suburban scenes were sought out, and the people in the bus were encouraged to get out and take photos.

'So they would see a tyre swan and stop for commentary and photographs,' I suggested.

'I imagine people would get quite angry, with a busload of people taking photographs of them,' Tim said. They would have had the reaction that the woman who owned the hotel in Bairnsdale, where we had stayed the night before, had when we asked if we could take a photo against the red and silver wallpaper in the dining room. She was completely and utterly confused, even offended.

'I don't know why you'd want to do that ... it's horrible wallpaper ... well, you've come here, done what you need to do, I suppose ... you got here so late last night ... I just don't understand.' Her reaction was as if she suspected us to have some sinister purpose behind taking the photo, beyond just liking the wallpaper.

After walking around for a while we stopped at a corner store, where a group of kids were bickering over what lollies to buy at the counter, the lollies that you buy loose and get in a small white paper bag. I quickly took stock of the store, I always expect to find great things in neglected aisles of corner stores, old merchandise you can no longer get, like Vegemite in toothpaste tubes and packets of Fags. The only mildly interesting thing I found was a great supply of dusty canned squid. I realised that the man behind the counter was staring at me suspiciously, so I joined Tim in buying a bottle of water. There was no Coburg Cola. We continued walking until we got to a street with tram lines, and we sat side by side on the wall hemming in a small park to discuss our next move. I checked where the trams went: the city. We decided to catch the next one and then ring Vic to plan what we were going to do that evening. I felt happily unconcerned for whatever we did next. I could have kept walking, kept sitting on the wall, gone back up to Sydney Rd and eaten more Tabet's, kept searching for Coburg Cola – anything.

After I found a seat in the stuffy tram I felt sleepy, I shut my eyes and did not pay attention to the unfamiliar streets we were travelling down. I could not rest very well because nearby two old uni chums who had met by coincidence were having a loud but very dull conversation about uni, work and obtaining Australian citizenship. I felt like commending them for keeping up such a boring conversation so loudly, for so long. Their talking made me feel even tireder, I looked wearily out at the housing commission towers with the primary-coloured window frames, and shook my head slowly when Tim asked 'Have we gone past the city?' I was relieved he thought the journey was taking a long time as well, I felt like I was being slowly cooked by the afternoon sunlight, and trams are so slow, I become very impatient when I am on one for more than a few stops.

Once we arrived in the city we got off at the stop near the library and crossed the road so I could use the payphone to call Vic. The twenty-cent coin I inserted became stuck and rattled in the slot vigorously, like an angry cicada. I bleated at Tim to help me, and while he was getting the coin out with a match I tried to use the phone on the other side, which did the same cicada thing to my coin. Once both coins had been retrieved we went to the next public phones, in the mall, where I complained that I would have to wait, as both were being used.

'Well we'll wait then,' said Tim, making me feel petulant. I was tired, and the nearby shoe store was blaring loud dance music, and I didn't feel much like ringing up Vic's relatives again. When I did he asked me to call him back in forty-five minutes, by which time he said he would have sorted things out, whatever that meant. We used this time by going to Collector's Corner to look at records.

'I just want to have a nap, then everything will be alright,' I said. 'I want to be able to go to a place where I can pay to spend an hour asleep.' A nap centre. I was disinclined towards looking at records because I was tired, I flipped through the new arrivals and then through the 10"s, trying to imagine what the songs were like on all the records that I didn't know, based on the photograph of the band on the cover, or the cover art. Two boys walked past me, one of whom dropped a small bottle of eye drops. His friend picked it up and said, 'Gonna have trouble seeing without these mate,' when handing it back. It seemed to me that eye drops were a peculiar thing to carry around, although it could be quite common, I have not paid much attention to eye drops in my life. For some people they are probably as crucial as black biros and particular notebooks.

I wasn't even really looking at the records as I flipped through them, so I told Tim that I would wait for him on the bench outside. My ankles were sore, I was suffering the exhaustion I always feel when on holidays, a combination of less than usual sleep, a lot of walking, and the stress of noticing so many details. I stared at the sign in the window about record 'stylii' being available, and it annoyed me even though it was grammatically correct. Styluses sounds much more human. I watched a guy with tattooed arms inspecting the Voivoid record he had just bought, until he noticed me looking and glared in my direction. When Tim came out of the store we went up to the ExeLoo, one of those modern automated toilets that Melbourne has a lot of. I called it the liaison facilitator, after we discussed how often people must have sex in them. The doors open after ten minutes but, as I said, 'you can do the preliminary work somewhere else, and then enter the Exeloo merely for the deed itself'. Tim looked around before he entered the Exeloo, saying, 'This is embarrassing.' When he was inside I realised what he meant, and started to laugh. The Exeloo was right in the centre of the pavement, exposed. I imagined the walls suddenly becoming invisible and how you would be stuck, indisposed, in the middle of the pavement. When Tim came out I was still giggling a bit, and I told him how the guy walking behind us had turned back to watch him enter the Exeloo with an amused look on his face.

'Prude,' I said, 'He can't accept natural body functions.' Tim explained how it had been pretty horrible inside the Exeloo, full of orange syringe caps and splatters of blood, so perhaps it would not be so good as a liaison facilitator.

I wanted to go and lie down in a park for a while because I was so tired, and suggested catching the tram to the park across from the art gallery, the stop for which was just where we were sitting. While waiting, Tim cut the offending label off the back of his new jeans with his fruit peeling knife. I offered to do it but when he stood up I felt self conscious about it, and so he severed the threads and ripped it off himself. It said something like 'Blues Union', one of those meaningless but annoying slogans the fastidious gent does not wish to display on the back of his trousers. With this done we caught the tram a few stops to the park. I pointed out the 'Ladies Only' seat outside the cathedral, and told Tim that it is the Melbourne meeting place for Steph and me. There was a guy sitting on the Ladies Only seat drinking a bottle of Solo with great gusto.

'He's got a hard earned thirst,' I said in my Voice of Dry Wit. Once the howls of laughter from my quip (the whole tram, as one, weeping with laughter) abated we got off at the park and crossed the street at the floral clock. The floral clock was not particularly floral, it was made up of various shrubs and grasses and said MELBOURNE across the top half of it. It was also five hours slow. There was a public phone across from it which I used to call Vic, and we decided to meet at the Esplanade Hotel in about an hour. With that organised, Tim and I went into the park to find a decent patch of grass for me to rest on.

A man ran past us, glancing back over his shoulder in a suspicious way.

'Doing a runner,' I announced, an old joke between Tim and me that anyone running is escaping from the law. When fifty metres behind him a group of angry men followed running and looking around them, and when we spied two police running behind them, and then more running men, we realised that this man had actually been doing a runner. I could tell that he was trying to escape from something from the slightly wild-eyed look he had when glancing back. We chose a half sun, half shade position on the grass, at the edge of the shadows from the tall surrounding trees. I lay down and shut my eyes and Tim got out his notebook and started to write in it. I couldn't relax very well so I opened my eyes again and watched the clouds of sunset insects, as small as dust motes, buzzing in messy spirals. I looked at the groups of people sitting on the grass nearby and the couples who paused in front of the statues to investigate them more closely. I felt peaceful and it was so good to finally be lying down that when we decided it was probably time to leave I couldn't stop myself from grumbling. After Tim attempted to ring his uncle from the payphone we crossed over to the tram stop and waited.

'Three minutes,' I announced, information which started Tim counting towards a hundred and eighty. I tried to distract him and make him lose count, but he clung on and reached his target.

'There,' he said, 'Three minutes takes longer than you might think.' The tram had not arrived and showed no signs of arriving. I turned to stare at the floral clock, and the person lining up a photograph in front of it. I saw the flash go off and imagined that photo being looked at years later. I have a cynical attitude towards such photographs, I would like to quiz people who take photos of, say, the floral clock, and ask them why they are doing it. If they said it was because the clock was interesting I would ask them to explain exactly in what way it was interesting. If they took a photo of people lying to form the hands of the floral clock or stealing one of the plants from the floral clock that would be alright, but otherwise it is merely some shrubs arranged in a pattern and two pieces of metal, indicating the wrong time. Two lots of people took photos of the clock while I was watching, so I can only imagine how many times a day the floral clock is photographed. I would like to erect a 'No Photographs' sign and see if this made people even more eager to photograph it, imagining they are gathering secret information.

On the tram Tim and I sat in separate seats and I stared at the people around me, while he stared out the window. I could hear two kids talking.

'Do you want to know the most impossible thing?' one asked. 'It's to be perfect. And the second most impossible thing is to speak another language when you don't speak it.' I was hoping that they would go through all the things they thought were impossible, but their conversation after this veered into the mundane, they started talking about shoes and bags and tram tickets. I stared for a while at a girl a few seats in front of me reading a book, noting the subtle changes in her expression as her eyes scanned down the lines of text. She furrowed her brow, then her face looked neutral, then her mouth curled up with a grin, then she looked confused. I imagined she must be reading something very interesting. Perhaps she knew I was watching and was putting it on. I decided this was probable considering how I often realise people are looking at me even if we have not made eye contact. The tram to St Kilda always feels as if it takes a very long time so distractions are welcome. The road that it travels down is lined with tall office buildings on separate blocks. This looks strange, as if the buildings in a city street have been picked apart with giant tweezers and placed in their own specimen boxes of landscaped gardens. When it was time to get off I gave Tim a nod and we stepped out onto the street outside the pub. Neither of us had been to the Esplanade Hotel, although we knew it by reputation.

We stood hesitantly at the bottom of the stairs, unsure whether to go in or not. A man staggered past and told us to go to the downstairs bar because it was better, at which point the security guard sitting on a plastic chair outside the entrance grunted his way into the conversation. I explained we were meeting someone inside and he suggested the larger upstairs bar would be a more likely meeting place. We chose to sit at a large table striped with bright sun. Tim bought pots of beer – after our initial reticence to order a 'pot' of beer instead of a 'schooner', although we knew that they are called 'pots' in Victoria it sounds wrong, and we expected to be laughed at – and we sat back and talked about the Find-a-Word I once made him on the topic 'Things that are Invisible'. He said he still had it, somewhere. I remember spending a long time writing a list of the most interesting things that are invisible: emotions, air, ghosts. I took the zine I had picked up from Sticky out of my bag. It was called *Yucky Yummy Food* and began with the explanation: 'Everyone has their own secret food, the stuff you eat when no one is around. The disgusting stuff.' Recipes included sandwiches with butter and Milo, hot chips inside burger rings and chips with jelly on them. We laughed at the serious style with which the recipes were explained, our own shameful food preferences unspoken between us. Chocolate cake and potato chips mixed together is a favourite of mine, for example. After we finished reading *Yucky Yummy Food* Tim went to find another payphone and I closed my eyes and listened to the conversations going on at the nearby tables. A woman was complaining about living in a house with no washing machine, a man was explaining how he could not stand the idea of a secondhand bed, another man was bragging about catching a shark.

'Well, I almost caught it,' he qualified, having got the attention of the table. 'There's a photo of it in the water beside the boat.'

I opened my eyes when Tim returned and we sat talking while keeping an eye on the entrance for Vic, who was now more than two hours late. Lateness is not unusual with Vic, but two hours was a lot, even for him. I turned around every minute or so, or if I saw anyone walk up the stairs out of the corner of my eye.

'If we start kissing,' I suggested, 'he will turn up. It will be the equivalent of lighting a cigarette to get the bus to come.' Tim laughed and leaned over and kissed me and, just as I predicted, twenty seconds later Vic walked up the stairs and into the pub. We were both laughing as he sat down at the table but he did not seem perturbed by this (usually when I have just walked into a room and sat down at a table of people laughing I feel a bit self conscious and want to know the joke, fearful that it is at my expense). He explained to us his tense visit to his grandmother's house, the clashes and snubbings involving various relatives.

'After I left it got better. I cleaned out the ute, I lined up everything in the back along the nature strip in a long line and I washed clothes and dishes and cleaned out the esky. Then I took Smith to Mentone and showed him where I grew up, and where I went to school when I was his age, and we went swimming at the beach.' I started to wish that I had come on this tour, I like to know such things about my friends. We stayed at the pub for a little while longer before leaving to get some food. Tim and I had been discussing what foods we felt like during the long wait for Vic to arrive, and I went into a dreamy spiel about noodles, how I could almost feel them in my mouth, thick wheat noodles with slippery sauce. I enjoy thinking about food so much, in fact some days it is the only creative thing I manage to come up with, what foods I feel like eating, and describing how they taste from memory.

It was cold outside, I wrapped my arms around my torso, feeling top heavy as I always do when I walk with my arms crossed. We walked to a restaurant we had seen from the tram, a vegetarian one with the definitions of the different types of vegetarians printed on the window. I ordered noodles and Tim ordered soup and I awaited them greedily. I snapped the disposable wooden chopsticks in two and pincered them between my fingers, ready, and I thought just how much I like self-serve cutlery and condiments, it is like taking control of your meal, choosing preferred implements and flavour enhancers. Tim gathered a range of cutlery, napkins and a bottle of soy sauce, which I drizzled over my noodles when they arrived, piled in the centre of a heavy white plate. Vic went off to the payphone (I have never used, or been in company of those who have used so many payphones so often at any other time in my life. Every spare moment was spent in the pursuit of a payphone) and Tim and I ate in relative silence, swapping plates back and forth so we could share. When Vic came back he had a few mouthfuls of soup but didn't look particularly interested in eating, perhaps because of his tooth problem. I polished off the rest of the soup Tim had left, and was picking individual noodles from the few left on my plate when I announced that we should go. I felt like I might soon start licking the plates and embarrassing myself.

I asked Vic for the keys to the ute, so I could get a jumper, and I walked to the car while they went to the (now ... guess)*. I carefully opened the back of the canopy and retrieved the red woollen shirt I had bought from Savers the day before. I stuffed it into my bag and took great pains to make sure the back of the ute was closed and secured correctly; I am bad with doors, opening them, locking them. Tim and Vic were walking down the street ahead of me, two tall, straight figures. Watching them I felt great love for both of them and felt lucky I knew them, when everyone else around had no idea that they were so unique and wonderful and interesting. I quickened my pace until I caught up with them. Tim was talking to his stepfather on the payphone and Vic was sitting on a low wall nearby. I lay down on the top of the wall and laughed when Tim told us his stepfather had suggested we go to find the 'world's largest fob watch. It is in Melbourne at the moment, you should go and see it'. I wondered just how big this fob watch was, picturing a huge one, sized for giants. We sat and talked about the watch for a while before deciding to go back to the Espy for more pots (familiar so soon). As we crossed the road I pointed out a Great Dane being walked in our direction. Like giant watches, I am in awe of giant domestic animals and was excited about the Dane's magnitude.

Vic and Tim looked at one another and said, 'That dog was really sexy. Did you see the way it was walking? Wiggling its hips? Like it was wearing high heels. It knew we were looking at it. Look how glossy and firm it is.' This

---

* *payphone.*

talk and various accompanying gestures continued as we walked down the street. I pretended to be outright shocked by this line of conversation, however I silently agreed. The dog had a very slutty, self conscious walk, one of those animals that seems so human in behaviour that it is disturbing.

We went back to the Espy and settled in the beer garden, after a few attempts to find a decent place to sit inside. We tried the downstairs bar, which was closing and full of very drunk girls, an abusive man who looked like a prison escapee and a couple pashing to 'Under the Bridge' by the Red Hot Chili Peppers. On the way back upstairs another couple asked me, 'Hey! What's goin' on?', a question I could think of no good answer to, so I just nodded. I pondered what, exactly, I could have said in reply and could think of nothing. To say the obvious, 'we're going to the other bar' sounded dull, but to say anything else, 'Just roamin' through the joint, man' (for example), was embarrassing. After this communication failure we sat inside, but the band was too loud for us to be able to hear one another talk so we went to the garden. It was better out there, we sat down at a table and I took out some of the larger articles in my bag to find my wallet. I took out Tim's camera and Vic said, 'I thought that was a high-heeled PVC boot.'

There was a moment of silence before Vic turned to Tim and said, 'Are you thinking about the dog?'

'Yes, but I was too shy to mention it,' Tim replied.

We didn't stay at the pub long, lured by the mysteries at the end of the pier. We left and crossed the street towards it. When we got there Vic and I both went to jump up on the wall that ran alongside the path so we could walk along it. We almost collided, but managed to miss one another skilfully. Tim hopped up on the wall as well and we walked along it in single file, swinging around the lamp posts when they appeared in our path. There were minor distractions as we walked: a poster with fish of the region displayed on it, which Tim inspected saying, 'I love pictures of fish'; a group of fisherman, one of which was eating fish and chips: a couple snogging and groping. At the end of the pier was the breakwater and we walked along that a little way before I protested exhaustion and sat down on one of the angular rocks that build up the side of the path. The other two sat down as well and we stared out silently at the horizon line, marked with blinking lights and the illuminated outlines of ships. I turned back to stare at the city and the blinking red lights that act as markers on the top of tall buildings, which I have always thought are put there so planes don't crash into them, although now thinking about it I am not so sure that is correct. We sat quietly until one of us suggested we walk back.

'I wonder if the couple are still there?' Tim said, but when we passed where they had been they were gone.

'Gone to make a baby,' I suggested, before laughing about how condom machines should be installed in the darkest corners of the pier. It had a weird feeling about it, a concrete road leading out into the water, lined with streetlights, with people dangling lines off the edge of it and people walking up and back along it aimlessly. We went back to the car, past a great number of buskers that were too close together to make any kind of individual impact – they were all men with guitars and small amps the size of encyclopaedias, singing in rough voices. The people on the streets looked drunker; the night seemed to be deteriorating.

I was pleased to get to the car, I sat in the back and rested my head against the window as Vic drove down the long, straight highway that lead to his aunt and uncle's house. The radio was playing hip hop, which seemed to fit the scenes going past outside the window, large stores selling the type of products that are not essential to life, but are nevertheless made to seem important by having such a large space dedicated to their sale. Aquariums, car accessories, hi-fi systems. We drove underneath a huge shopping centre with a bright, three-storey high walkway crossing the road. It looked like a giant fluorescent light. This was my landmark that indicated we were not far, and I closed my eyes for the rest of the journey, looking forward to settling down on the creaking camp bed and falling asleep.

Acknowledgements

Many thanks to the people who star in this book, who have been an inspiring influence on my life and writing: Patricia Berry, Fiona Berry, Stephanie Varga, Natasha Smith, Matt Curley, Vic McEwan, Kieran Carroll and Ryan Scott.

As zine writing is always a collaborative pursuit, I wish to thank the many people who have supported my zines, made zines themselves, written letters to me and been a part of the zine community. Special thanks to Kane Barwick, Miss Helen, Richard Vogt, Paul Vogt, Nicholas Carvan, Simon Yates, Sarah Coles, Leigh Rigozzi and Adam Ford.

This book wouldn't exist without Keri Glastonbury's enthusiasm and support. Thank you to her, Christen Cornell and the rest of LCP. For their assistance in the making of this book thanks to Keg de Souza, Pat Armstrong, Rachael Holt and Lucas Ihlein.

My greatest thanks go to Tim Wright, for being all of the above and much more.

Zines

A version of 'Relics' was first published in *I am a Camera* #6.
'Sometimes You Just Feel Like Spending Two Days as a Rabbit' and 'Turramurra Summer' were first published in *I am a Camera* #9.
A version of 'The Velodrome and the Olympia' was first published in *I am a Camera* #7.
'Postcards and the Colour Wheel' was first published as *I am a Camera #10.*

More information can be found at www.vanessaberryworld.com, or by writing to Vanessa at her Strawberry Hills post box.

Illustrations

Keg de Souza has her fingers in many pies. As well as illustrating, binding books and making zines, she is also an anarchitect, part of the Sydney-based artist/activist collective SquatSpace and founding member of NUCA: Network of UnCollectable Artists. Her website is: www.allthumbspress.net

Design

Strawberry Hills Forever was designed and typeset by Pat Armstrong. He is a Sydney graphic designer who cannot write about himself in the third person. www.somnambulist.org / pat@somnambulist.org

Quotations

'SCUM manifesto', Valerie Solanis, 1967, AK Press, 1996 edition.
'Little House on the Prairie', Laura Ingalls Wilder, 1935, HarperCollins, 1953 edition.

'A Journey into Deepest, Darkest Detail' was first published in HEAT 11, New Series, ed. Ivor Indyk, Giramondo Publishing Company, 2006.